Elm Leonard John Dufresne John Ed Bradley

Bobbie Ann Mason

Iy Duff Dee Brown Pat Conroy

Amy Bloom

eaney Cassandra King

ra (Malamud) Smith Kaye Gibbons

Anne Tyler

arnett Robert OConnor William Price

ed Nahui Coolugn O'B

Bebe Moore Campbell Carl Cateman

Clyde Edgerton

guie Shivers Clifton L. Taulbert

J. Buffett Bia Harm

Adriana Trigiani F. C. Boyd

Gloria Norris

esley McNair Tom Franklin

utt Lawrence Wells Ann Patchett

Rick Cleveland Youmon G. Koch

THE *New* GREAT AMERICAN WRITERS COOKBOOK

Alas, I have no real interest in cooking—only eating.

—RICHARD FORD

THE *New* GREAT AMERICAN WRITERS COOKBOOK

Edited by Dean Faulkner Wells

Foreword by Julia Reed

University Press of Mississippi / *Jackson*

www.upress.state.ms.us

Designed by Todd Lape

The University Press of Mississippi is a member of the
Association of American University Presses.

Manufactured in the United States of America

11 10 09 08 07 06 05 04 03   4 3 2 1
∞

Library of Congress Cataloging-in-Publication Data

The new great American writers cookbook / edited by
Dean Faulkner Wells.
    p. cm.
Includes index.
 ISBN 1-57806-589-5
 1. Cookery. 2. Authors, American—20th century—Anecdotes. I. Wells, Dean
Faulkner.
 TX715.N5217 2003
 641.5—dc21   2003006647

British Library Cataloging-in-Publication Data available

CONTENTS

PASTA, EGGS & GRITS

STEWS, SOUPS & A LOT OF CHILI

SEAFOOD

POULTRY & GAME

MEATS

SANDWICHES, BREADS & ONE CHEESE PUFF

DESSERTS

FOREWORD

by Julia Reed

Years ago, I flew to Michigan's Upper Peninsula to interview the novelist and poet Jim Harrison for a profile in *Vogue.* It is not an easy trek from Manhattan—requiring on this occasion a big plane, two little planes, and a rental car—but it turned out to be worth it. Harrison is a great interview, he became a friend, and perhaps best of all, he gave me a really, really good dinner.

That last part was a surprise—Harrison had only just begun writing the food pieces that would be collected in *The Raw and the Cooked.* A vague tip-off had come in the form of a message left with my assistant that I should bring some decent wine—but I didn't know if he needed enough to last him through the remainder of the winter, or just enough for our visit. So I compromised with all that I could carry on the plane, about eight bottles, and I'm pretty sure we drank them all. Fortunately, before we were well into it, he had cooked: thick pork chops that were brined first and then slowly grilled over charcoal, and a stir-fry of young asparagus, morels, and green onions he dubbed "Asparagus Julia." To kill the next day's hangover, there was a robust venison chili and some much-needed strong coffee.

Writers are well known for that business about drinking all the wine; their connection to cooking is not as, say, fundamental. They do cook though, and some do it really well—hence, the existence of this fine volume pulled together by Dean Faulkner Wells. Harrison, one of the "Great American Writers" included in this volume, says he cooks because he has lived most of his life in "the geography of the interior" (Michigan and, more recently, Arizona and Montana) and he is simply trying to replicate the great restaurant meals he has enjoyed and would otherwise be mostly deprived of. Harrison's friend Philip Caputo says he turned to cooking after his divorce out of necessity and kept at it because it turned out to be such a useful diversion: "It demanded so much concentration that I couldn't think of anything else—things like writer's block, royalty statements, deadlines, and bad reviews."

Diversions are important. Writing is such a solitary enterprise that, at the end of the day, making and/or breaking bread with others is often necessary to keep from going crazy. In *The Artists' and Writers' Cookbook,* a predecessor of sorts to this book, published in 1961, John Keats (the Canadian writer, not the English poet) supplies a lengthy breakfast menu, including sausage cooked in wine with lentils, French bread toasted with garlic butter, and cauliflower flavored with cider—enough, that is, to enable "people who work like dogs" all day to do it, so that when they're through they'll be able to enjoy a civilized dinner, complete with the necessary wit ("rather than humor") and companionship. "Work then, on a full gut," Keats writes. "This is life. And at evensong, a time for repose and reward. In a word dinner. . . . I strongly suggest that one should breakfast like a peasant, and dine like a viscount."

Writers are, by nature, full of such pronouncements. We have an irritating tendency to think we know everything about everything, including, of course, food. Lillian Hellman supplied a recipe for shrimp creole to *The Artists' and Writers' Cookbook,* along with a single observation: "Deveining shrimp is nonsense." (When I am simply cooking, I wholeheartedly agree with her. But when I am writing—or, more precisely, when I am on a deadline and, therefore, not writing—deveining shrimp is precisely the kind of task I would take up with great enthusiasm.) Anyway, in the same volume William Styron explains, at great length, how to properly create southern fried chicken, that "most put-upon, abused and generally misunderstood of all indigenous American culinary triumphs," and correctly asserts that "to 'deep-fry'—to immerse rather than properly to fry—is not to fry at all, it is to pickle." Jonathan Franzen feels equally strongly about the "Pasta with Kale" he has contributed to these pages, declaring that the addition of grated cheese would amount to nothing short of "a desecration."

Alice B. Toklas, Gertrude Stein's companion and the author of a wonderful cookbook/memoir (*The Alice B. Toklas Cookbook*), wrote in the introduction to *The Artists' and Writers' Cookbook* that the "Writers write like they write, and the painters write like they paint." The writers on these pages are similarly true to their styles. Elmore Leonard's instructions for making his "Southron Breakfast Treats" are as devoid of bullshit as his superlative prose: "Now open a can of Underwood Deviled Ham. . . ." Dave Barry's instructions for making "Toast with Peanut Butter" is full of his usual hilarious exaggerations and words in screaming capital letters; Clifton Taulbert's "Southern Peach Cobbler" is not so much a recipe as another of his moving memoirs of growing up in the Mississippi Delta—its ingredients include "courage and desire" and "a radio with the ability to still play the sounds of Ruth Brown and Hank Snow." And of course the author of a novel entitled *Slow Poison*, Sheila Bosworth, would provide this caveat with her recipe for "Crevettes Désir" (otherwise known in her native New Orleans as barbecued shrimp): "Never feed [it] to anyone in whose dreams, for good or ill, you are unwilling to remain forever."

Like Taulbert and Bosworth, most writers, while cooking at least, stay true to their roots as well. Only a Southerner would offer up dishes whose key ingredients are carbonated beverages (Mark Childress's classic "Coca-Cola Cake" and John Edge's fabulous-sounding "Blenheim-Spiked Sweet Potatoes"). The Southerners are also big on pies (Mississippian Gloria Norris supplies the recipes for "Lemon Icebox" and "Buttermilk"; North Carolinian Lee Smith gives one for "Bourbon Chocolate Pecan"), while Texans Anne Rapp and Jim Lehrer are partial to chili. Louise Erdrich, who currently lives in Minnesota and whose novels often center on the lives of Native Americans, tells us how to cook "Wild Rice for a Lot of People" with rice cultivated by the Obijway.

There is also ample evidence that the relationship between writer and booze remains a thriving one. Chris Offut's "Kentucky Breakfast" consists entirely of "steak/bourbon/ and a dog/to eat the steak." Mark Richard's "Recipe for a Hangover Cure" sounds so good—and is written so well—it makes me want to go out and tie one on just so I can try it. Larry Wells, the novelist who also happens to be married to the editor, helpfully provides another hangover solution, a "Nutritious Bloody Mary" with a wedge of lime, whose "shiny green rind . . . implies Vitamin C." Bloody Marys also play a part in Andrei Codrescu's "Transylvanian Shrimp Creole"—but they are not to be added to the dish itself, required instead "for mood." Harrison's frame of mind is similarly enhanced. "It is unthinkable to cook without drinking wine while doing so," he writes. "In fact, my motto is, 'Drink wine or someone will drink it in your place.'" This is not something Styron would have approved of—at least not while making his own fried chicken. "Without discipline," he warns, "without attentiveness—nothing. You cannot go into the other room and booze it up with your waiting guests."

While many of the writers in this volume resort to the sound practice of mining their mothers' recipe files, it is obvious that some are also serious cooks in their own right. There is Harrison, of course, whose prodigious kitchen talents—and lustful approach toward the business at hand—are evidenced in his "Posole from Sonora." But then it doesn't take a cookbook to get Harrison going on food. In just two pages of his beautiful long poem, "The Theory and Practice of Rivers," he manages to mention venison with truffles, an ambitious *bollito misto*, a perfect, just-caught brook trout, and lists pretty much all the makings for that restorative Spanish stew, *menudo* ("about ten pounds of tripe, ancho, molida, serrano, and chipotle pepper, cumin, coriander, a few calves' or piglets' feet").

Padgett Powell is another of the few American writers who mention food in their work, and here he has produced a peerless primer on the making of gumbo, along with some excellent "Cracker-Yucatan Ribs" inspired by the ur-authority on Mexican cuisine, Diana Kennedy. I'm impressed with anybody who mentions Kennedy's name, but I already knew Powell was no novice in the kitchen. A few years ago, while reading his novel *Edisto Revisited*, I had to get up out of my bed and go to the grocery store to buy the makings of a chicken club sandwich. The protagonist had made one for his girlfriend, and Powell so brilliantly evoked that salty-tart thing that makes the sandwich so alluring that I couldn't stand it until I'd eaten one myself. On subsequent pages I was further tantalized by descriptions of "soft scrambled eggs" with "heavy pepper" served with neat whisky, and the excellent pairing of a Smithfield ham with a gin and tonic (it's that salty-tart thing again).

But Powell is not the norm. Most American literature is seriously devoid of culinary references. Which is why it is such a pleasure to read Tolstoy. Proust may have written a million words based on memories prompted by a simple teacake, but the madeleine really was not the point. In *Anna Karenina*, on the other hand, Oblonksy (Anna's jolly brother) is so obsessed with food that it becomes almost another character. He is forever planning menus, confabbing with waiters, "peeling the sloshy oysters back from their pearly shells with a little silver fork and swallowing them one after another." He revels in the joys of "a superb but simple roast beef"; he forces sauces and chablis on poor simple Levin. It is at one of his massive hors d'oeuvres buffets—featuring cheeses and caviar, pickled mushrooms and various preserves, French bread and six kinds of vodka—that the successful reunion of Levin and Kitty is facilitated.

In American fiction, those coming close to Oblonsky's obsession most often seem to be detectives. There is the vast and fussy gourmand, Nero Wolfe, and there is Lawrence Sanders's more appealing Delaney of the Deadly Sin series. The man cannot eat enough sandwiches. He eats "interracial sandwiches" including ham on a bagel and "wet sandwiches" like the delicious-sounding potato salad and pastrami on rye with hot English mustard. (Even the people he's chasing eat them. *The First Deadly Sin* opens with a health conscious serial murderer munching on stone ground whole wheat with radishes and plum tomatoes.) And then there's Patricia Cornwell's intrepid medical examiner and, apparently, culinary alter ego, Kay Scarpetta. The recipe "Kay" provides in these pages, "Miami-Style Chili with Beer" comes from the novel *All That Remains*, where it was made by Kay's friend Anna.

Of the other cooks/writers in this book, I can attest that Curtis Wilkie knows his way around a stove because, fortunately, I am his neighbor and he's made his justifiably famous pasta dishes for me many times; I have also been lucky enough to have had Jimmy Buffett grill me a bluefish one night in Bridgehampton, and I highly recommend his marinade. And I have had the enormous pleasure of dining many times with the fine writers and insatiable gourmands Johnny Apple and Jay McInerney, with whom one always eats and drinks extremely well.

Of course, if you're a writer by profession, it is better to be able to write than to cook. If you're good, after all, you can still make a gripping narrative out of the trying. Witness

Howard Bahr's "Hopping John," which is essentially an essay on not being able to cook, or Tom Franklin's "Chubb Stew." I'm not sure I'll ever make the stuff (though it's hard to pass up a dish whose broth contains three of my favorite drinks, coffee, Dr. Pepper, and beer), but I was truly sorry when he was done making his. In the end, a writer may wax more poetic with the pen than the whisk. Roy Blount's memorable "Song to Grits" is an homage to their healing power: "When my nerves get frazzled, When my flesh gets loose—What knits me back together's grits." In *Jericho*, James Dickey pays similar tribute to okra: "You talk of supping with the gods. You've just done it, for whom but a god could have come up with the divine fact of okra?"

Katherine Anne Porter wrote wonderful descriptions of the food she ate growing up in Texas, but I don't think she ever wrote an ode to the dishes closest to her heart, and I know William Faulkner didn't. But sometimes a mere few words suffice. Eugene Walter told a famous story about Porter and Faulkner dining together in Paris, at someplace swell, possibly Maxim's. They had polished off dinner and a bottle (or, more likely, two or three) of Burgundy when Faulkner looked up and said, "Back home the butter beans are in, the speckled ones." And Katherine Anne Porter just looked off in the middle distance and said, "Blackberries."

FROM THE EDITOR

This is a cookbook for all tastes in food—and literature—with recipes as varied in style as the poets, novelists, journalists, playwrights, essayists, and screenwriters who penned them. Many are straightforward, serious, mouth-watering dishes. Others are flights of fancy, or perhaps fantasy, each a delight, which gallop the gamut from tofu to heart-clogging chili, from gourmet "Sonoran Stew" to "Stuffed Camel" (in case you need to serve four hundred; prep time *two days*). One contributor requested that his recipe be printed with a coupon for a complimentary angioplasty.

There are standard recipes as well as essays—tributes, treatises—on food. Some writers legitimately borrowed recipes from trusted sources, while others—by their own admission—have shamelessly stolen. Some of the non-cooks offer suggestions: "How to Get Your Wife, Mother, Husband, Friend (take your pick) to Do the Cooking for You." I also could not resist including some disclaimers: "I cook no better than Mr. Toad drove his motorcar in Grahame's *Wind in the Willows*."

The recipes have been reproduced just as the writers submitted them. Editorial meddling has been kept to a minimum. If your favorite writers are not included on these pages, please give the editor the benefit of the doubt. She tried to reach them and shares your disappointment in her failure.

Editing this book has been a privilege and a pleasure. I dedicate it to the writers with respect, admiration, and gratitude.

Thank you,
DFW

BEVERAGES, APPETIZERS & CONDIMENTS

I cook no better than Mr. Toad drove his motorcar in
Grahame's Wind in the Willows.

—DEAN KOONTZ

LAWRENCE WELLS

is the author of the novels *Rommel and the Rebel* and *Let the Band Play Dixie*. He also wrote an Emmy-winning TV documentary, "Return to the River," and contributes to the New York Times Syndicate. He lives with the editor.

Nutritious Bloody Mary

This is a full-bodied Bloody Mary born in collusion with Willie Morris in Oxford, Mississippi, during the 1981 college football season. We wanted a Bloody with the illusion of wholesomeness to combat hangovers and lend hope that the Ole Miss Rebels could beat Georgia. The recipe has been tested on sportswriters from the *Clarion-Ledger,* the *Commercial Appeal,* and *USA Today.*

Football weekends usually kick off at 5 P.M. Friday and pep-rally into Saturday. Mid-morning on game day as the crowd drifts in, I have been known to open cans of tomato juice in my sleep. Plain, high-quality tomato juice. Don't use V-8 unless you think vodka tastes good with the combined juices of beets, parsley, spinach, and watercress.

The Nutritious Bloody was first served at our kitchen table (the hub, the center) where sportswriters congregated, seeking nurture the morning after. I fixed drinks at the kitchen counter. Willie, seated at his favorite kitchen chair with his back to the wall, tested the first Bloody while toying with the notion that losses build character.

A famous drinker once wrote that a Bloody Mary is not doing its job unless you can see through it. Don't stint on vodka (one and a half to two ounces per glass, depending on the size of the drinker), but Bloody Marys were never meant to be a pink martini. The hangover crowd demands thick, red glassfuls with healthy-looking things floating around.

I mix Bloody Marys by the glass. Go to pitchers and you're on your own.

Lots of lemon pepper, a bit of celery salt. (Fresh celery stalks optional.) Splash of Worcestershire sauce. Squeeze a lime wedge and drop it in. Its shiny green rind implies vitamin C. Tabasco is of course essential. Three shakes of the bottle, maybe another. Dab of horseradish to open the sinuses. Whole ice cubes, not cracked.

Stir. Drink. Talk football.

Lawrence Wells

LINTON WEEKS

was born in Memphis. He is a staff writer in the Style Section of the *Washington Post*. He was the founding editor of *Southern* magazine and managing editor of the *Washington Post Magazine*.

An Extreme Gin and Tonic

In an iced tea glass, pour a couple of ounces of gin, as good as you can afford. Add plenty of ice. Start slicing your fruit to give the ice a little settling time. Add fresh tonic water to taste, but leave room in the glass for the juice of ⅛ grapefruit, ¼ orange and ⅓ lemon. Then squeeze the juice of ⅓ lime into the glass and run that raggedy wedge around the glass rim twice.

Stir and say ahhhh.

This is not an old family recipe. My family didn't drink. But it comes from *Southern* magazine, a magazine I once ran and loved. We billed this recipe as the perfect drink for the contemporary South—somewhere between sin and salvation.

Linton Weeks

DEAN FAULKNER WELLS

is the editor of this cookbook.

Pappy's Whiskey Punch

This punch was served to celebrate the Faux Faulkner Contest. My husband, Larry, and I coordinated the contest and hosted the party at our home in Oxford. The consensus choice of a fitting beverage was this sour-mash punch. We learned, the first year, that adding three cups of whiskey guaranteed instant bonhomie. At the end of the party, guests were observed drinking from the punch bowl. The second year we cut back on the whiskey, but found ourselves refilling the punch bowl twice as often. For the occasion I took the liberty of renaming the punch in Pappy's honor.

    1 quart cranberry juice
    2 cups pineapple juice
    1 cup orange juice
    3 cups Jack Daniel's Tennessee Whiskey
    1 quart ginger ale

Combine all ingredients and pour over a cake of ice in a punch bowl. Garnish with fresh cranberries, orange and lemon slices. Makes about 28 servings.

LISA NEUMANN HOWORTH

has published *The South: A Treasury of Art and Literature* and *Yellowdogs, Hushpuppies, and Bluetick Hounds: The Official Encyclopedia of Southern Culture Quizbook.* She lives with two dogs, four cats, three children, and a mayor.

Purple Teelolly: A Refreshing Sparkling Cocktail

My bud, the renowned screenwriter Anne Rapp (see page 96), says that this recipe was first conceptualized when she and I and Laurie Stirratt, renowned bass player for Blue Mountain, were sitting around in the Two Stick Bar, and the two of them, being single ladies, were lamenting the sorry array of available and appropriate men, and plotting, I think, to jump, I mean encourage, a couple of the inappropriate ones. Later, Davell Crawford threw a fiftieth birthday party for me, and he and Anne mixed up a big batch. It quickly disappeared, and nobody would own up, but a bunch of people went home suspiciously early.

Mix well: 1 gallon cranberry juice, 1 bottle Stoli (because it's distilled with the passion and despair of the Russian soul), 2 physicians' sample packs Viagra (12 little blue nubs), crushed.

Serve over ice and a splash of soda, but not to chirren, unsuspecting guests, heart patients, guys wearing speedos or on duck hunting trips, or fewer than a dozen people.

MARK RICHARD

won the 1990 PEN/Ernest Hemingway Foundation Award. His work includes *The Ice at the Bottom of the World, Fishboy,* and *Charity: Stories.* He lives in California and writes for television.

Recipe for a Hangover Cure

(no substitutions)
1 large old banana, black-stemmed and spotted but not rotten
1 quart fresh orange juice
4 generic aspirins, crushed with the butt of a loaded pistol
1 bag convenience store ice
2 tablespoons wheat germ
1 large shot of raw honey
3 dollars
1 large ocean, chilled

Attain consciousness. Sit on edge of bed and stare at feet for fifteen minutes. Put on anything that's obviously yours. Go to Hardees or McDonald's and buy a sausage, egg, and cheese biscuit and also a cinnamon raisin biscuit. Go home.

Into blender put whole banana, then fill blender near to top with ice. Sift in the aspirin. Spoon in the wheat germ and squirt the shot of raw honey. Fill the blender with the fresh orange juice. Blend until mixture is free of ice gravel and smooth, but do not overblend into runniness.

Pour half the blender into a plastic stadium cup and sip a little. Open bag and take out the two biscuits. Savor the grease and crisp edges of the sausage, egg, and cheese biscuit but do not eat more than half. Sip some more from the stadium cup. Eat as much of the cinnamon biscuit as possible. Finish stadium cup and pour rest of blender into cup. Feed remaining biscuits to the dog.

Go down to the ocean, sipping. Set down stadium cup and wade into surf. Dive in and swim down hard until the pressure of about twelve feet of water crushes in on your skull, stay down until you almost pass out, and scramble up to the surface and enjoy the pressure leaving your head, the highly oxygenated air filling your lungs. Stagger out of the surf and sit on beach, looking out to sea. Finish stadium cup, feel momentarily better, then weep and pray for a sober reckoning of your soul, miserable sinner.

LEE K. ABBOTT

is the author of six collections of stories, most recently *Wet Places at Noon.* He teaches at Ohio State University in Columbus.

The Late Johnny Brownfield's Heart-Cloggin' Chile con Queso

1 box of Velveeta (the big 'un, amigos)
1 humongous red onion (no smaller than a heavyweight's fist)
4 cans chopped green chile
6 to 8 pinches of garlic salt
4 to 6 generous dribblings of Tabasco
2 tablespoons of milk (skim, 2%, whole—shoot, it doesn't matter)

Melt that railroad tie of cheese-like material in a big sauce pan (I like to microwave because I'm always in a hurry, and there's less chance the stuff will burn, which results in matter brown and algae-like; purists, or those embarrassed by even the idea of Velveeta, will probably hire this stage out).

When stuff gets gooey, even drippy, throw in (from across the room, if necessary) the chopped chiles, green not red (Old El Paso brand is well nigh everywhere available; fresh, of course, is better, but durn few of us actually live in Hatch, New Mexico, home of the best; if, however, you do have the real deal on hand, be sure to remove the skin off the roasted pods; otherwise, you're in for some interesting, and not at all mouth-watering, mastication).

Let the stuff simmer for a time (during which you can shred/slash/burn any evidence that you've actually bought and will shortly consume vast quantities of a comestible from the Spam, Vienna sausage, margarine, pimento loaf, and Butter by the Squirt family of foods).

Chop that onion—not too finely, though; after all, you do want something to sink the teeth into. And you must use red. You do want color, no? Toss in the garlic salt according to taste. Ditto the Tabasco (or Louisiana Lightning, or Hell's Kitchen, or The Sweat of Satan, or House Afire—in short, whatever hot sauce you're enthralled to). Once more, it's simmer time and the living is easy, during which half-hour you begin arranging the corn chips (the bigger, the better) in the shape of your current state of mind. Cast your eye upon your handiwork. Sing a song of six pence. Draw the blinds. Unplug the phone. Dress in plastic.

Finally, add the milk. (Why milk, you're wondering, to which I, and history's high-dollar philosophers, can only answer: Why not? This is the recipe Brownie gave me, ingredient for ingredient, back when we were teenagers and I had found myself in Deming, New Mexico, chopping cotton for the summer with a galoot named Ears and dating a DHS Wildcat sweetie named Eeef. Brownie lived on a cattle ranch midway between Deming and the Twilight Zone—yes, the middle of nowhere, heaven the only landmark to hope for—and had a little sister, Martha-call-me-Muffy, I might have otherwise sparked. He and I shared a best friend, Ernest "Ernivac" Richard Green, and no little affection for the comely half of our crooked kind, not to mention considerable, albeit juvenile, interest in anything written by Leon Uris. Brownie liked to put his queso on eggs; me, I developed a fondness for slathering it on bread—white, of course. Heck, it might likewise be an acceptable alternative for mortar or joint compound or sunburn ointment. In any event, Brownie died last year—no, not from an affliction associated with eating what you're about to—and I can't think of a better way to honor his memory than to imagine innocent Americans everywhere sitting down to a tubful of the tastiest con queso a gringo not named Wolfgang can cook.)

Refrigerate the leftovers. Has, so far as anyone has discovered, the shelf life of coal.

L— K. Abbou

WESLEY MCNAIR

has held grants from the National Endowment for the Arts and from the Rockefeller, Fulbright, and Guggenheim Foundations. He has also received prizes in poetry from *Poetry, Poetry Northwest,* and *Yankee* magazines, as well as the Sarah Josepha Hale Medal. The kitchen his wife, Diane, refuses to let him enter is located in Mercer, Maine.

Hot Mustard

½ cup dry mustard
½ cup cider vinegar

Mix until smooth. Let stand overnight.

Beat 2 eggs lightly. Add ⅓ to ½ cup sugar (brown or white). Mix with mustard and vinegar. Heat in double boiler until thick.

In the bad old days, when I worked the early shift and came home to take care of our four kids so my wife, Diane, could work nights, my only evidence she was still alive were the notes she left on the stove about what to cook for dinner. Sometimes they said "fr. fr. and fish sticks—cole slaw in fridge," sometimes "warm up spag. sauce in pan." She had learned from experience to keep my involvement minimal. In my one fling at cooking I invented a dish called "Rufus Porter Stew," named after the country muralist of the nineteenth century who traveled New England with brushes, sponges, and crude stencils, making primitive murals that contained hunters with dogs, sedate colonial houses, steamboats, cigar-shaped islands, and volcanoes, in a mix of perspective that was all wrong and somehow just right. My stew, a combination of hamburger, whatever happened to be ripe in our vegetable garden, and spices by whim, was all wrong, too—all wrong period. Not even the dog would eat it.

Diane being the only cook in the family, I asked her to produce a recipe for this occasion that neither of us could live without. The one she handed me was "Hot Mustard," its ingredients listed on yellow-lined paper in the handwriting of our best friend. Even if you'd never tasted the concoction, you'd be able to tell it was good just from the way long use and the ingredients themselves had smudged the ink.

From that time-honored document, written from one friend to another, I've copied the recipe above for the readers of this book. The mustard that results goes best with a plate of pretzel sticks, a pitcher of beer and, yes, friendship. Cheers.

Wesley McNair

SARAH CRICHTON

is a writer and editor in Brooklyn, New York, where she lives with her husband, writer Guy Martin, and their daughter, Eliza Grace.

Mary's Curried Chicken Salad

For my first married Christmas, my mother-in-law in Alabama sent me a country ham to prepare for her son (see page 91). When I uncrated the thing, it was furry with mold, so I tossed it. I grew up on New York's Upper West Side; how was I to know that was the way it was supposed to look? In those early days of marriage I tried to give my Southern husband the foods he was missing. I baked a batch of corn bread, but I added sugar to it, which appalled him. Only Northerners put sugar in corn bread, he said. I tried to make cheese grits, but not only was the cheese wrong, the grits were wrong, too. He tried to be sweet about my forays in regional cooking, but he always wound up slightly let down, and in time I had to face this fundamental truth: It's a foolish woman who tries to serve her husband the foods his mother used to make.

This chicken salad belongs to no particular tradition of cooking whatsoever. It's very light because it's made with crème fraiche, and works well as an hors d'oeuvre for cocktail parties, in multiple quantities for a large lunch crowd. It also makes a helluva sandwich.

> 6 skinless, boneless chicken breast cutlets
> 1 cup crème fraiche (see page 165)
> ⅓ cup mayonnaise
> 1 tablespoon curry powder
> Salt to taste
> 4 heads Belgian endive (optional)

1. Poach chicken breasts by simply putting them in a heavy, covered pot. Do not add any liquid or oil. Just put them in a pot, cover, and cook over a low heat for about 20 minutes. The chicken breasts will poach in their own liquid. When cooked through, remove from the pot and let cool for a few minutes.
2. Using your hands, pull the chicken breasts apart and shred into feathery pieces.
3. Combine crème fraiche, mayonnaise, and curry powder, and then toss the chicken with the curried dressing. Salt according to taste.

4. For hors d'oeuvres, serve chicken salad in endive leaves, like little boats. For lunch, serve with a good chutney. If a wetter, more dense chicken salad is desired, add more mayonnaise.

—Sarah Crichton

KENNETH HOLDITCH

is Research Professor Emeritus from the University of New Orleans and founding editor of the *Tennessee Williams Journal.* He is the author of *The Last Frontier of Bohemia* and co-author of *Tennesse Williams and the South,* a pictorial history.

Barney Barnhill's Eggplant Appetizer

Brown 1 lb. ground beef and drain off fat.
Add seasoning:
Chopped onion
Chopped bell pepper
Chopped celery
Chopped garlic
Italian seasoning
Thyme, fresh or dried
Mushrooms
Lemon zest
(Optional: tomato juice)

Salt a cubed eggplant and let it stand for a while; then drain and add to meat mixture. Saute for about an hour until all the flavors meld.

Serve with crackers, toast rounds, or French bread rounds.

The recipe for this wonderful appetizer was given to me by a colleague at the University of New Orleans, Viron L. Barnhill, who was a Cajun and a great cook. It is always a favorite when I serve it to guests—and I can hardly stop eating it myself.

CATHIE PELLETIER

is the author of *The Funeral Makers, Once upon a Time on the Banks, The Weight of Winter* (winner of the 1992 New England Book Award), and *Dancing at the Harvest Moon* (under the pseudonym, K. C. McKinnon).

Ethel's Mustard Pickles

    30 pickling cucumbers
    1 large onion
    4 or 5 pickling jars (large ones)
    ⅓ box pickling spice
    Brown vinegar
    Salt
    Cotton rag or cheese cloth
    1 cauliflower
    4 heaping tablespoons cornstarch
    2 tablespoons dry mustard
    l tablespoon tumeric

You'll need a large pan. Cut the cucumbers and the onion into bite-sized pieces. Layer the cucumbers with onion and salt until your pan is full.

Let it sit overnight. Drain, and then add enough brown vinegar so you can see it through the cucumbers. Put ⅓ box pickling spices in piece of cotton rag and tie securely. Add ½ of a 5-pound bag of sugar and cook to boiling.

Cut up cauliflower into bite-sized pieces and blanche (cook to boiling), then add to the pickles.

Thickening Ingredients
4 heaping tablespoons cornstarch
2 tablespoons dry mustard
l tablespoon tumeric

Mix these three ingredients with enough brown vinegar to make a thickening paste, and then add this to your pickles to thicken them. Fill your jars, seal, and enjoy the best pickles in the world!

My mother's name was Ethel Tressa O'Leary Pelletier. She was born and raised in St. John, Maine, before coming to even more remote Allagash in 1935, as a house helper when she had finished high school. That's how she met and married my father, Louis. Her mother, Augusta McKinnon O'Leary, taught her how to make these pickles, a recipe passed down from my great-great-grandmother, Elizabeth Gardner Moir. I suspect it came from Elizabeth's mother, Anna Diamond Gardner, who was a Loyalist who came to Allagash from New Brunswick, Canada, in 1835.

I don't remember the first time I tasted Mama's mustard pickles. As a child, I used to help her pick the cucumbers each year from her garden. She always made enough jars to get us through a long, cold winter in northern Maine. After I left home and roamed about, Mama would always mail me a few jars each year, knowing how much I loved her pickles. The jars went through customs while I was living in Toronto and Moncton. By the time I'd settled in Tennessee, my mailman would hear the clinking jars inside the box and say, "I think your mother sent you some of her pickles." Then he'd come into my kitchen, I'd open the box, and we'd sit and eat mustard pickles. I went back home for a time to take care of Mama, when she became ill with cancer. She died December 27, 2000, in the same house where I was born. Even the air feels different without her in my life. My sisters and sisters-in-law are the ones who make her mustard pickles now. The last time I was home, I noticed a few dusty jars down in the basement, sitting on the rickety bookcase my brother Vernon made back in grammar school. No one has the heart to open them, so I guess they'll always be there, Mama's last pickles.

Cathie Pelletier

JOHN T. EDGE

contributes articles to *GQ, Gourmet,* and *Saveur* and is a columnist for the *Oxford-American.* His cookbook, *A Gracious Plenty,* was nominated for the James Beard Award. He is editor of the series *Cornbread Nation.* He lives in Oxford, Mississippi.

Deconstructed Pickled Peaches

Inspired by a lack of time and energy
Peaches
Best balsamic vinegar
Turbinado sugar
Cracked black pepper

Peel and slice peaches. Pour on a healthy glugg of vinegar and a grind or two of pepper and a bit of sugar. Allow to macerate for an hour or so. Serve with a sprig of mint if you have it.

LEE SMITH

won the 1999 American Academy of Arts and Letters Fiction Award. Her work includes *Fair and Tender Ladies, Saving Grace, Me and My Baby View the Eclipse,* and *The Last Girls.* She lives in Hillsborough, North Carolina.

Holiday Cranberry Chutney

½ cup cider vinegar
2 ¼ cups firmly packed light brown sugar
¾ teaspoon curry powder
½ teaspoon ground ginger
¼ teaspoon ground cloves
¼ teaspoon ground allspice
½ teaspoon cinnamon
2 lemons, rind grated, pith discarded, and fruit cut into sections
2 naval oranges, rind grated, pith discarded, and fruit cut into sections
1 apple, peeled and chopped coarse
6 cups cranberries, picked over
½ cup golden raisins
½ cup chopped dried apricots
½ cup chopped pecans

1. In large saucepan, combine vinegar, sugar, curry powder, ginger, cloves, allspice, cinnamon, and 1 ½ cups water and bring liquid to a boil, stirring until sugar is dissolved.
2. Add lemon rind, orange rind, lemon sections, orange sections, and apple, and simmer mixture, stirring occasionally, for 10 minutes.
3. Add 3 cups cranberries, raisins, and apricots, and simmer mixture, stirring occasionally, for 30 to 40 minutes, until thickened.
4. Stir in 2 cups remaining cranberries and simmer, stirring occasionally, for 10 minutes.
5. Stir in remaining 1 cup cranberries and pecans and simmer mixture, stirring, for 15 minutes.
6. Transfer chutney to a bowl, let cool, then chill, covered, overnight or for up to 2 weeks.
Yield: 6 cups

Lee Smith

SALADS &
VEGETABLES

The trouble with me is I'm not a cook. I don't have any kitchen procedure that is recommendable to anybody except eating.

— WENDELL BERRY

STEVE KLUGER

is a novelist and playwright. His books include *Changing Pitches* and *Last Days of Summer*. He wrote the stageplays *Bullpen, After Dark,* and *Pilots of the Purple Twilight.* He lives in Santa Monica, California.

Below, the recipe. I figured I might as well present it in character. . . . [from *Last Days of Summer*]

The Charlie Banks Bean Salad
(like I would know what to do with an oven even if they gave me one which they don't)

> 1 can of chick peas
> 1 can of kidney beans
> 1 can of corn
> 1 can of string beans
> 1 jar of mushrooms
> 1 jar of pimentos
> 1 Bermuda onion
> Oregano
> Salt
> Pepper
> White vinegar
> Balsamic vinegar
> Olive oil

First you open up the cans and dump everything into a bowl. Then you chop up whatever's supposed to be chopped up in case it already isn't (like the onion and the mushrooms and the pimentos and etc.). Then you throw that in the bowl too. Then you shake in some salt but not too much. Oh yeah and pepper—but also not a lot. And then oregano—the more the better, even if flakes get between your teeth. And then finally white vinegar and balsamic vinegar and a little bit of olive oil. (I don't think it is as dangerous as it sounds, though I would not want to light a match around it.) Then you put it all away and forget about it for two days. It is like cold spaghetti and meat loaf before it turns green. It always tastes better when it is older.

But how come they are asking me????? It is like asking Julia Child to play left field.

Very truly yours,
Chas. Banks, 3d Base
NY Giants

ALAN LIGHTMAN

is the author of the novels *Einstein's Dreams* and *Good Benito*. His novel *The Diagnosis* was a National Book Award finalist. He is an adjunct professor at the Massachusetts Institute of Technology.

Spinach Salad a la Kitty et Fred

¼ cup white vinegar
¼ cup oil
2 tablespoons chutney
2 teaspoons sugar
2 teaspoons salt
1 ½ teaspoons curry powder
1 teaspoon dry mustard

2 tablespoons sliced scallions
10 ounces spinach
1 ½ cups chopped apple
½ cup raisins
½ cup peanuts

Combine ingredients and shake well. Pour over salad.

Alan Lightman

PATTY FRIEDMANN

is the author of *Eleanor Rushing, Odds, The Exact Image of Mother,* and, most recently, *Second Hand Smoke.* She lives in New Orleans.

Sweet Jamie Joy Slaw

She had big yellow hair and big red lips and she wanted to write erotica. Jamie Joy took my workshop three times, and all she produced was one short story in which the male protagonist resembled Buddy Holly, three workshops full of frustrated men, and this recipe. I'd take it over erotica any time.

2 ½ cups grated carrots (about 6 to 8)
2 ½ cups thinly sliced red cabbage (about ¼ medium head)
½ cup mayonnaise
½ cup granulated sugar
Salt (to taste)
Fresh cracked black pepper (to taste)
½ teaspoon Tony Chachere's creole seasoning
Juice of 1 lemon
½ cup raisins

Place carrots and cabbage in large bowl. Fold or mix in all the other ingredients except raisins.
Bring 2 cups water to a boil. Turn off, drop raisins into water, let sit 5 minutes. Drain off water. Fold raisins into mixture in bowl.
Chill and serve. Makes 4 servings.

ANNA QUINDLEN

received a Pulitzer Prize for her work as a *New York Times* columnist. She is the author of *Being Perfect*, *Object Lessons*, *One True Thing*, and *Blessings*.

Anna Quindlen's Summer Pasta Salad

8 to 10 very ripe tomatoes
6 big fresh basil leaves, minced
¼ cup red wine vinegar
1 cup good olive oil
Juice of one lemon
1 lb. spaghetti
Ground pepper

In the morning halve tomatoes and squeeze out seeds. Cut into small cubes. Put in a big jar (an empty mayonnaise or large mason jar will do). Add all ingredients except spaghetti. Shake hard and put on a sunny windowsill, shaking again from time to time.

In late afternoon boil spaghetti. After draining dump into a bowl. Dump the jar contents on it and toss.

Serve at dinner when the salad is more or less cold. You can make this with fried chicken and not have to serve anything else unless you have fancy guests, and you shouldn't have fancy guests in summertime anyhow.

Anna Quindlen

MARK CHILDRESS

is the author of five novels: *A World Made of Fire, V for Victor, Tender, Crazy in Alabama*—for which he also wrote the screenplay—and *Gone for Good.* He lives in New York and New Orleans.

Dude's Macaroni Salad

There are lots of good cooks in our family. You just have to check out our waistlines to be sure of that. But the best, by general acclaim, is Miss Dude Cranford of Greenville, Alabama. Dude is one of those natural cooks who never seem to measure anything, or look at a recipe book, but whatever she cooks always comes out great, and there are never any leftovers. I would try to tell you how Dude makes the world's finest buttermilk biscuits, but I've been trying without success to duplicate these biscuits for years.

These days, editors at fancy food magazines are beating down Dude's door for her recipes. Dude doesn't claim to have originated these recipes but I know she has put her own magical touch on them.

The macaroni salad, she declares, is "really good, and you can put it with any kind of meat. We like it with spareribs." It also contains that magic ingredient without which all recent Southern home cooking would disappear—a can of cream of mushroom soup.

1 8-ounce package elbow macaroni
1 lb. New York State sharp cheddar cheese, grated
¼ cup chopped bell pepper
1 small can pimento peppers, sliced, for color
1 small can mushrooms, whole or sliced, either one
1 cup mayonnaise—Blue Plate if you can get it
1 can cream of mushroom soup

Cook macaroni according to package directions. Mix it well with all the other ingredients and ¾ cup of the cheese. Sprinkle the remaining ¼ cup of cheese on top. Bake at 350° for 45 minutes, until bubbly and brown.

JAYNE ANNE PHILLIPS

was nominated for a National Book Critics Circle Award for her novel *Machine Dreams.* She is the author of *Shelter, Fast Lanes, Black Tickets,* and *From Motherkind.* She lives near Boston.

Thornhill Double-Boiler Potato Salad

This is my mother's recipe and she was famous for it, but it's not for those fearful of heart attacks.

To the cook: The secret is in the dressing; it's really a cooked sauce. But first, make the potato salad. Understand that the recipe doesn't work to full power unless you are very precise about cutting the pickles, olives, onions, and eggs into perfect little cubes, like my mother did. Then be patient about stirring the dressing.

Combine in a large bowl, all chopped small except potatoes:
10 (peeled) large, boiled potatoes, firm but done through
1 dozen hard-boiled eggs, fully cooked
1 lb. (crisp fried, unburned) bacon
1 large onion, chopped fine, or 2 bunches green onions with stems
Small bunch chives, cut fine
1 large jar green olives with pimento
2 large sweet dill pickles, chopped fine
1 large jar mayo
1 tablespoon of bacon grease
2 tablespoons red wine vinegar
½ teaspoon dill weed
Salt and pepper to taste

For the dressing, mix in double boiler, no heat:
2 eggs
2 teaspoons flour
2 teaspoons mustard
½ cup vinegar
½ cup water
¼ cup butter

Then cook, stirring, in double boiler until consistency of hollandaise. Pour over salad and stir gently.

LOUISE SHIVERS

is the author of *Here to Get My Baby out of Jail*, which was named Best First Novel of the Year by *USA Today*. Her novel *Whistling Woman* received the Georgia Author of the Year award. She lives in Augusta, Georgia, where she is a writer-in-residence at Augusta College.

Mother's Potato Salad

Written by my mother, Julia Shingleton

About five large or medium potatoes. Peel potatoes and cut in fairly small cubes. Boil in salted water until tender. They cook in a few minutes. I use small handfuls of salt because being well seasoned is the secret of a good salad.

Drain in colander if you have one and let cool.

To the potatoes, I add desired amounts of chopped bell peppers, chopped onion, three or four boiled eggs, chopped, and as many celery seeds as you like. Mix all together with mayonnaise. I never use salad dressing.

Sprinkle small amount of paprika over top for looks if you have it.

This is famous in the large Shingleton family. People who don't usually like potato salad beg for this. We joke about the Yankee men who marry into the family, say "no thank you" when the platter is first passed, and after a taste, start driving hundreds of miles for their own dish. We also have a young relative who lives in Tennessee and is known across the mountains as "the girl whose grandmother makes that potato salad!"

Louise Shivers

KENNETH HOLDITCH

Biographical statement, p. 12.

Christian's Cold Beef Salad

Chuck roast
3 carrots, big pieces
Bay leaf
3 scallions, whole
Celery
Beef bouillon
Pepper (no salt)
Thyme
Clove of garlic, chopped
1 large onion, quartered
Turnip
2 marrow bones

Put chuck roast in big pot and barely cover with cold water. Add other ingredients. Boil for 2 ½ hours. Cool. Slice meat when cold.

Add:
1 scallion, chopped
Salt and pepper
Oil and vinegar

Toss and let stand ½ hour or longer.

This recipe was given to me by the late Christian LeFebure, a Frenchman who became a professor in New Orleans. He always served it with boiled potatoes marinated in beef broth and tossed in oil and vinegar and chopped green onions. It is a wonderful recipe for summer, since it can be made ahead and is served at room temperature.

TERRY KAY

is the author of eleven novels, including *To Dance with the White Dog* and *Taking Lottie Home*. His most recent work is *The Valley of Light*. He is the eleventh of twelve children. His mother was a renowned cook in northeast Georgia.

Tomato Pie

I first had this wonderful tomato pie at the home of my dear friend Camilla Watson, who was kind enough to share the recipe with me. I, of course, had to tinker with it, in much the same manner of an editor working over a manuscript. It's a must-do thing, and in that regard, cooks and editors have more in common than cooks and writers. In this recipe, the tinkering is acknowledged by italicized lines.

> Unbaked pie shell *(Pillsbury, the kind you unfold)*
> 3 or 4 large tomatoes
> 1 medium chopped green pepper
> Salt and pepper to taste
> 1 teaspoon of dry basil
> Garlic powder to taste
> ¾ cup of Hellmann's mayo
> ¾ cup of grated sharp cheddar cheese
> ¾ cup of grated Swiss cheese

Unfold pie shell into dish. Bake for 10 to 12 minutes at 350°. Peel and slice tomatoes. When pie shell has baked for 10 to 12 minutes, remove from oven. Place sliced tomatoes in pie shell. *Sprinkle chopped green pepper over tomatoes.* Add salt, pepper, basil, and garlic powder. Mix cheese and mayo together and spread over tomatoes. Put in oven at 350° and bake for 30 to 35 minutes.

Note: *The original recipe did not call for chopped green peppers, but I like the taste and even like a little mildly hot pepper (like a mild banana pepper). Also, the original recipe called for sharp cheddar cheese; I mix cheddar (sharp, medium, or mild) with grated Swiss. A suggestion: Don't be afraid of using more basil, since basil and tomato are perfect together. Be generous with garlic powder if you like garlic; and though the recipe calls for mayo, don't forget the salt.*

Terry Kay

HOWARD BAHR

served as a gunner's mate in the U.S. Navy in Vietnam. He is the author of *The Black Flower, The Year of Jubilo,* which won the Mississippi Institute of Arts and Letters Award, and *Home for Christmas,* a children's book.

Hopping John and Other Fables

First off, I should make it plain that I'd as soon do long division as cook. I hate the art and all that pertains to it, and I do not practice it. Furthermore, I have little use for eating and would not do that either, save when I don't, I get peckish. All who know me will be astonished to find me in a cookbook, but no more astonished than myself. In any case, I am honored to be among such distinguished company, whatever the venue. Now I can say, "Yes, Barry (or Larry, or Ellen, or Amy, etc.) and I worked on a book together." I can claim that it was nothing unusual, that we do it all the time, and so on. It would not be as big a lie as some I have manufactured.

And now, from the man who cannot make a grilled cheese sandwich, comes a venerable dish I have prepared almost every day since I was weaned more than half a century ago. The cooks of the U.S. Navy did not include it in their repertoire, so I went those four years without it, but I was young then and could suffer any hardship. In the Southern vernacular, the dish is known as "Hopping John," though in my family it was, and is yet, known as "Peas and Rice," or *Le Pois et Riz.* I use the French because it seems more . . . chef-like.

To succeed, the ambitious cook must first master *Le Riz Parfait,* or "The Perfect Rice," a secret handed down to me by my good friend Dr. Randy Cross, who learned it years ago in the monastery, and which I now give to you. It is an important process, for rice is a staple in the Southern American diet, as well as that of China, Japan, and Southeast Asia. Think about that for a moment, then begin.

Prime: Buy a box of Uncle Ben's Converted Original Rice. I do not pretend to know how it can be converted and original at the same time. In any event, read the instructions on the side of the box and follow them.

Seconde: The crucial element is to cover *le pot* and let *le riz* simmer for 20 minutes—no more nor less. Do not be tempted, as so many are, to lift the cover and look inside to see what is happening. Nothing is happening of any interest. Neither may you stir. Go away and occupy yourself at some useful thing until the 20 minutes is up, then set *le pot* aside for 5 more minutes. You still can't look. At last, in due season, lift the lid and *Voila!: Le Riz Parfait*!

Tierce: Open a can of Bush's Best Black-Eyed Peas. Put them in *l'autre pot* and boil on high—no use fooling around.

Quatrieme: Put some of the rice on a plate and put some of the peas on top of it. Mix them together. Serve with bacon, Spam, Red Devil Potted Ham, or some other easily prepared side. Drink ice (not *iced*) tea (in the French, simply *The*—I do not think they have a word for ice).

I am gratified to be able to share with the general public this simple, but robust, dish. My present constitution is owed in large measure to it; I can only hope it may do the same for others.

ELIZABETH MITCHELL

is the author of *Three Strides before the Wire: The Dark and Beautiful World of Horse Racing* and *W.: Revenge of the Bush Dynasty.* She lives in New York.

Hungarian Stuffed Cabbage (Family Recipe)

Some of you will see the words "stuffed cabbage" and keep flipping by. You will probably imagine for a moment those pallid logs lying in a pool of watery broth at cheap Polish diners. Some of you will never even cross the pages of this recipe, skipping, with the aid of the index, directly from "honey-baked ham" to "icebox cake," or what have you. You will be wrong. And this recipe will lurk in the book like the brittle, acid heart of a Hungarian, slighted yet again.

I inform you of this inevitable outcome as a knowing descendent of the Magyar people. If your grandfather hitchhiked on a boat from Hungary as a teenager with nothing but a few embroidery skills, and your grandmother was the child of Czechs who lived close enough to the border to make the ancestry a quibbling detail, and if your mother and her six brothers and sisters still try to read aloud the postcards from the Miskolc relatives at Christmas Eve dinner, and if one of the childhood games taught to you, and now your nieces and nephews, involves mumbling Hungarian incantations over a child's trusting palm, while you softly stroke your finger along the life line, then the love line, until crack! you sever the tenderness abruptly with a stinging slap, and if you can sing the old folk song in the native tongue, the first line of which translates as "you are pretty in the face," the likelihood is you know the nooks and crannies of the bruised and cautiously brutal Hungarian heart.

That is to say, you should not skip this recipe because you will hurt the feelings of Hungarians everywhere. But you should also try it because, when cooked in just the right way, this food will addict you. Intensely flavored rolls, smothered in sauerkraut sweetened through long cooking, and bolstered by paprika and tomato, this dish is best enjoyed with a bottle of Egerian Bull's Blood.

As far as I know, this recipe was published only once before, as part of a benefit cookbook for the symphony in the hometown where my grandfather settled alone while still a teenager, eventually married the much-younger Czech girl, had seven children, lost the girl to cancer when some of the brood were still young, accumulated an ice-cream parlor, opera house, pub, and several houses while still a tailor, and then died—all of those properties disappearing from the family holdings like the steam off boiled cabbage. This is where I grew up.

In my copy of the cookbook, my mother has crossed off the word "beef" in "2 to 3 pounds ground beef" and penciled in "pork." My brothers and I tease her that she wanted the locals to have her recipe, but no hope of mastering it. Pork is the way to go.

Also note that the sour cream is for my mother the equivalent of recommending a digital video recorder. The idea was introduced to us by a local boy of Hungarian descent in the eighties, and despite the distrust lurking in the Hungarian heart, my mother tested the condiment on the cabbage and now we would never go back to having stuffed cabbage just "plain."

My mother makes *töltött kaposzta* better than anyone, but if you pay attention to the roux, browning the onion as dark as it will go without burning, you may come close to her perfection. The parenthetical remarks in the recipe are hers.

2 to 3 lbs. ground pork
½ cup uncooked rice per lb. of pork
Salt
Ground pepper
Green cabbage
1 large can sauerkraut
1 large can tomato juice
1 tablespoon sugar
Large onion
2 tablespoons butter
2 tablespoons flour
Sour cream (optional)

Cut core from cabbage; parboil cabbage just until leaves are pliable. Mix uncooked ground pork, uncooked rice, salt (approximately 1 teaspoon per pound of pork). Cut hard spine from cabbage leaves; cut leaves in half if they are large. (Small cabbage rolls are more appealing.) Place small quantity of pork and rice mixture at outside edge of cabbage leaf. Roll up and tuck ends into roll. Lay rolls on bed of sauerkraut in large Dutch oven/pot until all the mixture is used. Top with sauerkraut. Sprinkle with sugar and more salt and pepper. Pour tomato juice and small amount of water to top level of rolls. (Looks like a lot of tomato juice, but blends with other ingredients.) Cover and simmer for 2 hours on top of stove. Brown minced onion in butter in frying pan. Add flour to make roux. Add roux to cabbage roll pot (rinse frying pan with little water and also add to pot). Continue to simmer for another hour or more. (This roux adds special dimension to stuffed cabbage.) Serve with or without dollop of sour cream. (Flavor enhanced second day.) Yield: Each pound of meat mixture makes approximately 8 rolls.

THOMAS HAL PHILLIPS

has received the O. Henry Award and two Guggenheim fellowships. He collaborated in writing the screenplays of Robert Altman's *Nashville* and *Thieves Like Us*. He lives in Corinth, Mississippi.

Squash Souffle

   3 ½ cups cooked, mashed squash
   ½ cup milk
   ¼ cup sugar
   4 eggs
   2 sticks of oleo
   ½ cup flour
   1 small onion, chopped
   Salt and pepper to taste

Cook squash to ¾ done. Add finely chopped onions. Cook until tender. Drain and mash. Add other ingredients to squash mixture. Pour into buttered casserole dish. Bake at 350° for 30 minutes or until done. Will rise when done.

JOHN T. EDGE

Biographical statement, p. 15.

Blenheim-Spiked Sweet Potatoes

Inspired by my favorite not-so-soft drink, Blenheim ginger ale.

   2 sweet potatoes, sliced ¼ inch thick
   1 bottle Blenheim's ginger ale
   Butter
   Salt
   Pepper

Dot the bottom of a casserole dish with butter. Layer slices of sweet potato in an overlapping fashion. Sprinkle a bit of salt, a grind or three of pepper. Pour one bottle of Blenheim's ginger ale over the top. Bake for approximately one hour at 350° or until the potatoes are brown and the sauce is caramelized.

LOUISE ERDRICH

is a poet and novelist. She won the National Book Critics Circle Award for *Love Medicine,* a collection of poetry. Her work includes *The Last Report on the Miracles at Little No Horse* and *The Master Butchers Singing Club.* She lives in Minnesota with her daughters.

Wild Rice for Lots of People

1 lb. Ojibway harvested Wild Rice, available from

> White Earth Land Reclamation
> P.O. Box 327
> White Earth, MN 56591

2 yellow onions
1 jar chopped sundried tomatoes in oil
½ lb. sunflower seeds
Broth
3 cloves garlic (or more to taste)
basil, if you like

Wash rice until the H_2o comes clean—remove bits of hull that float—use a Dutch oven if possible and fill with water or broth to first thumb knuckle while touching the rice itself. (I don't know why this works.) Put broth cubes in to taste if you don't have the good homemade kind or canned.

Boil rice 30 to 35 minutes, then gradually turn down heat. Saute your onions. Set aside. Peel garlic and add while rice boils. Toast your sunflower seeds in a cast iron skillet.

Once rice is fluffy add seeds, onions, oil, and tomatoes and stir around—done. Basil is optional—fresh, chopped.

Louise Erdrich

BARBARA BUSH

is a former first lady and mother of President George W. Bush. Her books include *Barbara Bush: A Memoir, Grassroots Women: A Memoir of the Texas Republican Party,* and *Millie.*

Baked Beans

- 2 cans (16 ounces) small baked beans
- 6 tablespoons catsup
- 1 tablespoon Worcestershire sauce
- 3 tablespoons dark brown sugar, packed
- 1 teaspoon dry mustard
- 3 tablespoons grated onion

Bake partially covered in a 2 ½ quart casserole at 325° for 1 ½ hours.
Serves 6 to 8.

Barbara Bush

ROBERT LOVE TAYLOR

is the author of *Loving Belle Starr, Lady of Spain,* and *The Lost Sister.* He has taught at Bucknell University and co-edited the literary journal *West Branch.* He lives in Mifflinburg, Pennsylvania.

Appalachian Stir-Fry

Get a bunch of colorful vegetables at Food City or Kroger's, preferably in the summertime when everything is coming in from nearby and not shipped from California and waxed up. I like fresh broccoli, red and green bell peppers, celery, a big yellow onion, and purple or violet cabbage. Choose whatever is bright and beckoning. If there is fresh garlic available, get some. Then select some chicken parts. Personally, I prefer dark meat, and thighs are frequently on sale, but the more expensive boned white meat is easier to slice (tip: buy the meat a day before you mean to cook it, then freeze it and slice it up the next morning—it's easier to slice, and then you can marinate it for the rest of the day).

The chicken, after it is cut into strips, should soak in a mixture of soy sauce, sherry, and hot sesame oil or Tabasco for at least several hours. Experiment and vary the mixture to your taste.

Rinse off those beautiful vegetables, chop them up, peppers into strips, onion into chunks, and put them aside.

Pour a little oil, maybe a couple of tablespoons' worth, in the wok (a big skillet will do). Personally, I don't think it makes a lot of difference what kind of oil—corn or peanut or, if you're feeling lavish, olive—but I add something spicy-hot to it such as hot sesame oil, and then, when the oil is sizzling hot, anoint it with finely chopped garlic.

Next remove the chicken from its marinade and toss it into the hot and garlicky oil. When the chicken is done—about 4 or 5 minutes—remove it and set it aside. Stir in the fresh vegetables, onions first, and cook for 4 or 5 minutes, stirring frequently. Don't cook them too long. You want them crisp. When the vegetables are right, promptly return the chicken to the wok and add your glaze, which can be a half-cup mixture similar to the marinade, but with a teaspoon or so of cornstarch stirred into it. Stir the chicken, vegetables, and glaze for a minute, no longer, not to make everything soggy. Now serve with rice and, on the side, a well-iced can of Pabst Blue Ribbon, one per guest, with extra in the icebox. Without the Pabst is okay, but not true Appalachian.

STEPHEN CALDWELL WRIGHT

is a professor at Seminole Community College. His poetry collections include *First Statement, Poems in Movement, Urgings and Sayings, Talking to the Mountain, Out of the Wailing,* and *Nearly Exactly.* He received the International Poets Academy Award in 1988.

Uptown Country Casserole

My friends and relatives accuse me of not sharing my recipes: this simply is not true. Of course, they also accuse me of not sharing every little detail: in this matter, they are correct. Isn't this law written somewhere?

Fresh broccoli
Boneless chicken parts (thighs or breasts)
Campbell's Creamy Chicken Mushroom Soup
Assorted cheeses
Butter
Chopped onions
Lawry's Garlic Salt and Parsley
Lawry's Pinch of Herbs

Cook 1 package of chicken in deep pot with ½ stick of butter and ¼ cup of chopped onions. Sprinkle Lawry's Garlic Salt and Parsley and Pinch of Herbs, to taste. When chicken is done, slice into bite-sized portions.

Add 2 cans of creamy chicken mushroom soup. Bring to boil. Add 2 cups of chopped, assorted cheeses (cheddar, mild and sharp, recommended). Stir until mixture is even. Add chopped fresh broccoli and stir until mixture is even.

Pour into deep baking pan and sprinkle with paprika. Bake in oven at 350° until slightly browned.

DAVID GALEF

has published nine books, including *Flesh, Turning Japanese, The Supporting Cast,* and *Laugh Track,* a short story collection. A displaced New Yorker, he is a professor of English at the University of Mississippi.

How and Why to Prepare *Hiyayakko*

To the outsider, the varieties of Japanese cooking may seem like the difference between rice and rice. And not everyone likes sushi, which in any case can be rather expensive, especially for an expatriate just getting by in Japan by teaching English lessons. *Hiyayakko*, which a Japanese friend once described as "frozen white cube," is quite cheap and nutritious. A tofu-based dish, it's one of the glories of Japanese summer cuisine, though it can be enjoyed any-time you scare up the ingredients.

Directions:

1. Spend some time as an expatriate in Japan (not required but helpful). Those Sunday mornings walking around the downtown mall in Osaka when everyone else is either win-dow-shopping as a couple or in groups of thirty on a school trip make you feel both lonely and hungry.
2. Purchase a block of newly made tofu, or as fresh as you can get it. When I lived in Nishi-nomiya, I would wander over to the *tōfu-ya* to gaze at the wares floating in a tank, like somnolent blocky white fish in an aquarium. That's the kind of tofu, silky and custard-like, you can eat straight from the carton if you like.
3. Gather scallions, soy sauce, ginger root, and *katsuobushi*—this last ingredient, dried bonito flakes, which look just like pencil shavings, is everywhere in Japan but hard to get outside a specialty shop in the United States. Acceptable substitutes are canned tuna or sardine scrapings, which approximate the taste and humility.
4. Chill the tofu in the refrigerator, then lay it flat on an attractive oblong plate, if possible, for the proper Asian feel. (Japanese *senryū:* "European cookery: / every damned plate / is round.")
5. Mince scallions and grate finger—I meant to type "ginger," but you'll probably add some finger into the recipe if you get distracted. Scatter bits of scallion and ginger over the block. Sprinkle *katsuobushi* or its equivalent on top. Add a dollop of soy sauce.
6. Cut tofu into bite-sized squares. Consume with chopsticks, which can be challenging to do, considering how slippery tofu is. With a small bowl of rice, that's lunch. Repeat until sick of this dish and move on to miso soup.

SHAY YOUNGBLOOD

is the author of *The Big Mama Stories* and the novels *Soul Kiss* and *Black Girls in Paris*. She was the 2002–2003 John and Renee Grisham Writer-in-Residence at the University of Mississippi. She is not a vegetarian.

Southern Fried Tofu Alexander

1 package of extra-firm tofu
Drain and pat dry the tofu; cut into ¾ inch slices, then triangles.

Dry mix:
Fine corn meal
Spike
Curry powder
Salt
Dried cilantro or parsley
Paprika

Marinade:
Juice from ½ grapefruit
Juice from ½ lemon
2 cloves of garlic, mashed

Marinate tofu slices in juices and garlic for an hour or more in the refrigerator, turning once.

Dredge slices of tofu in dry mix and fry in ½ inch of hot olive oil. Brown and cook till tofu reduces slightly in size. Drain on brown paper.

When I told my friend Daniel Alexander Jones (poet, performance artist, theatre director, master chef, and longtime vegetarian) that I thought tofu tasted like carpet padding, he gave me this recipe. "Southern Fried Tofu Alexander" satisfies my Southern sensibilities for deep fried and delicious.

Shay

PASTA, EGGS & GRITS

I don't even know how to scramble an egg, while my wife, though an excellent cook, doesn't have any particular favorite recipes of her own. Hers come from other cookbooks, and to cite them as her own would be highly un-cricket.

— LOUIS D. RUBIN JR.

PHILIP CAPUTO

is a former prize-winning correspondent for the *Chicago Tribune*. His books include *A Rumor of War, Horn of Africa, Del Corso's Gallery, The Voyage, Ghosts of Tsavo,* and *In the Shadows of Morning.* He resides in Connecticut.

Why I Learned to Cook: Phil's Mom's Lasagne

I grew up in a traditional Italian-American family. That means I learned two things early in life: 1. Eating well is the best revenge. 2. The kitchen is no place for a man, except when he's sitting down to breakfast, lunch, or dinner.

To make a quantum leap in time, I got married in 1969 and had a traditional marriage for the next twelve and a half years. My wife took care of the children and the house, and did all the cooking while I made a living. Jill was (and still is) a very good cook, so I continued to eat well but remained more ignorant about cooking than I was about differential equations.

The marriage ended in divorce in 1982. It was a traditional divorce. Among other things, she got the house, including all kitchen utensils. I moved into a three-room cottage, which had a small galley kitchen in which I felt as alien as an atheist in church. Overnight, I stopped eating well. Cornflakes and ham sandwiches became the mainstays of my diet at home. Because I was paying hefty alimony and child support, I could not afford to eat out except at places whose menus offered that style of cuisine I call "Haute Truck Stop."

Also, Jill and I had shared custody of our boys, Geoffrey and Marc, who were playing junior-league football at the time and had appetites the satisfaction of which caused one to think of feeding time at the Lion House. I was required to fill their insatiable stomachs every Friday to Sunday, an obligation I fulfilled with daily visits to McDonalds, Burger King, and those ghastly eateries that advertise themselves as "family restaurants." Family restaurants have salad bars—always a sign of dreadful fare—but cheap prices. Nevertheless, I ended each weekend about $125 poorer. That would have been bearable if I'd been, say, a stockbroker, investment banker, or Stephen King; but I was not a mega-selling writer, ever haunted by the spectre of financial collapse. There was only one way out—I would have to forget my traditional, patriarchal upbringing and learn to cook.

I went to my local bookstore, and instead of buying the new novel for which John Updike had won his 45th Pulitzer Prize, I picked up the latest by Julia Child and the *Joy of Cooking.*

I got a C in high-school chemistry and flunked it in college. For the first few weeks, my attempts to put the *Joy of Cooking* into practice were, well, joyless and inept; you have to imagine Richard Nixon trying out *The Joy of Sex*. My sons, victims of my early attempts, rebelled against the custody agreement and preferred to remain with Mom on weekends. If I was to see them again, I would have to progress beyond Napalmed Hamburger. I watched cooking shows, read more cookbooks, and practiced. I made a discovery—even though I wasn't good at it, I liked cooking. It was relaxing because it demanded so much concentration that I couldn't think about anything else—things like writer's block, royalty statements, deadlines, and bad reviews.

To make another quantum temporal leap, I am today a fairly good hand in the kitchen. Geoff and Marc have grown into healthy young men without any signs of childhood malnutrition or food poisoning, and my new wife, Leslie Ware, a career woman, appreciates not having to cook every night of the week. Guests at our dinner parties do not gag or flee when I prepare the meal. I have to thank my mother, Marie Ylonda Caputo, who was my mentor through my long apprenticeship and taught me more than Julia and all those TV chefs. One of her favorite dishes is lasagna. I learned the recipe from her, she learned it from her mother, Enrichetta Napolitano, who learned it from her mother, Serafina Blasi, who learned it . . . well, the genealogy probably would read like Genesis 5 if I traced it all the way back.

My mother is an instinctive cook who eschews measuring cups and measuring spoons, to say nothing of more advanced devices and instruments. A pinch of this, a handful of that, a sprinkling of something else is as precise as she gets. Because America remains an Anglo-Saxon culture, despite the massive immigration from non-Protestant countries, and because most Americans don't have my mom's intuitive genius, the following recipe gives quantities of ingredients in nice, neat, numerical terms. But they are mere approximations of Marie's handfuls and sprinklings and pinches.

There are two secrets to this recipe. Patience and good ingredients. Anyone caught using Wisconsin milk mozzarella in place of imported buffalo mozzarella, or a bottled sauce instead of one prepared from scratch, will be sentenced to eat WASP-prepared Chicken Surprise for one year.

1 lb. lasagne (You can make it yourself, but store-bought kinds are OK and will not result in the above-mentioned punishment.)
3 to 4 lbs. fresh Italian plum tomatoes, peeled and crushed, or 2 cans of plum tomatoes
2 lbs. whole-milk ricotta cheese (No skim, please!)
½ lb. buffalo mozzarella
½ lb. freshly grated Parmesan
½ lb. pork neck bones

¼ lb. ground beef

2 eggs

8 to 10 fresh basil leaves, finely chopped

1 tablespoon oregano

3 cloves garlic

1 medium to large onion

2 tablespoons freshly chopped parsley

1 carrot, peeled

4 tablespoons extra virgin olive oil

Salt and freshly ground pepper

The Sauce

Heat 2 tablespoons of olive oil in 3 to 4 quart pot. Finely chop the onion and 2 garlic cloves and lightly saute in the hot oil until onion is clear and garlic is golden brown. (Do not burn the garlic.) Add tomatoes, chopped basil, oregano, two teaspoons of salt, pepper (6 to 8 twists of the mill), and the carrot. (The carrot "sweetens" the sauce by absorbing some of the tomatoes' acidity.) Stir well and bring to a boil, then turn heat down to very low and simmer, preferably for 6 to 8 hours, but no less than 4 to 5 hours. Approximately 1 hour before the sauce finishes cooking, brown the ground beef and pork neckbones in 2 table- spoons of oil, drain off fat and residue, and add to the sauce.

The Filling

You can prepare this anytime while the sauce is cooking. Shred the mozzarella and set aside. Cream the ricotta with ½ cup of grated Parmesan, 2 beaten eggs, chopped parsley, and 1 clove of finely chopped garlic. Salt and pepper to taste. Meanwhile, bring 3 quarts of water to a rolling boil, add the lasagne, and cook until al dente (about 10 minutes for packaged pasta, half that for fresh). Drain. (A tip: to stop the lasagne from cooking in its own heat and to make it easier to handle, throw ice cubes on it while it drains and shake well in the collander so it doesn't stick together.) Then lay out the noodles on a large board, a counter, or any other dry, clean surface.

Assembly

Preheat oven to 325°. Remove neckbones and carrot from the sauce. Ladle some sauce over the bottom of a large glass or foil baking pan. Place lasagne noodles *lengthwise* on the sauce, spread ricotta mixture over the lasagne, shredded mozzarella over the ricotta, and then more sauce over the cheese. Place the next layer of lasagne *crosswise* (trimming the ends if necessary), spread ricotta, then mozzarella, then sauce on it, add a third layer of pasta *lengthwise,* and repeat. Keep doing this, criss-crossing the layers of pasta, until it's *finito.* Put sauce on the top layer, but do not add the cheeses. Bake uncovered for 20 minutes. Sprinkle shredded mozzarella (but not ricotta mixture) atop the lasagne and bake for another 10 minutes. Remove from oven and let cool for 15 minutes before cutting into serving-size portions. Serve with garlic bread and extra sauce on the side.

    Serves 6 to 8.

Tip: The lasagne will taste even better if you prepare it a day ahead of time, refrigerate it overnight so it steeps in the sauce and cheese mixtures, and then reheat it (45 minutes at 275°) before serving. Once you've eaten this, you'll know why the Italian army has such a poor combat record: the soldiers are too stuffed and happy to fight.

Reviews: This dish got a third-helping rave from the novelist-poet Jim Harrison, one of the most exacting chefs and gastronomes I know. (See page 66.)

WYLENE DUNBAR

was a philosophy professor and lawyer in Oxford, Mississippi, before writing her first novel, *Margaret Cape*, winner of the Mississippi Institute of Arts and Letters Award. She has recently completed her second novel, *My Life with Corpses*. She lives in California.

Secret Sexy Spaghetti Sauce

This is a very powerful and potentially dangerous recipe. It was given to me by Dwight Ball, attorney-teacher-bon vivant, who created the sauce. He asked only that I keep it a secret and use it judiciously. So, please don't give out the recipe and prepare it only for someone with whom you would feel comfortable naked.

2 large cloves fresh garlic, very thinly sliced
1 medium Vidalia onion, chopped
1 large slosh red wine, or maybe 2 sloshes
1 pinch of sugar
2 large jars Prego Traditional Spaghetti Sauce (no substitutes!)
2 large jars Green Giant sliced mushrooms, drained
1 package of Hormel Hot and Spicy pepperoni slices, separated
2 cups water

Combine preceding ingredients in large pot. Heat. Meanwhile, prepare meat.

2 lbs. ground round
Dehydrated onion
Red wine
Extra virgin olive oil

Put a tablespoon or two of the olive oil in a 10-inch skillet and add red wine to make thin layer. Sprinkle dehydrated onions over top to cover. Press ground round over top to completely cover. Brown bottom of meat on medium heat, cut into wedges and flip meat over, breaking it up to complete browning. When meat is completely browned, drain and add to sauce. Simmer, uncovered, over low heat for 3 hours, adding water as necessary to keep sauce at desired consistency.

Serve with a good cabernet, hot French bread and a tossed, green salad. Serves 2 for an entire weekend, or one meal for 6 very friendly people.

EDWARD COHEN

is the author of *The Peddler's Grandson,* which won the 2000 Mississippi Institute of Arts and Letters Nonfiction Award. For many years he was head writer for Mississippi ETV. He lives in Venice, California.

Expatriate-Style Basil Spaghetti

Living six blocks from Venice Beach, where chainsaw jugglers and roller-blading guitar-playing turbaned Sufis are tame stuff, one becomes hardened. However, one thing I've never gotten used to is the absence of dead-summer Mississippi tomatoes. There's something about intolerable heat and choking humidity that produces the ripest sweetest reddest tomatoes on earth.

So I've had to adapt to local custom and produce, just as my immigrant grandfather did when eating kosher-style (i.e., with his eyes closed) catfish. The following spaghetti (not "pasta") dish has gotten me through several rough culinary patches.

One pint Cabo San Lucas cherry tomatoes (mixed red, yellow, and orange), halved. (If California-style tomatoes are unavailable, you may, without regret, substitute height of the season normal southern tomatoes. In the winter or when incapacitated, I've resorted to canned tomatoes, well drained.) The more tomatoes the better (within reason).

Put tomato stuff in bowl.

Chop a good bit of fresh basil and add to tomato stuff. (Back home in years past, particularly in the winter, I have had to resort to dried basil. Do this only if desperate.)

Extrude or finely dice one good-sized clove of raw garlic into compote. This is essential. When I'm feeling low or have a cold, I use two cloves.

Add salt and fresh-ground pepper. Cover the sauce with extra virgin olive oil. Not too little or the spaghetti will be dry (especially if you've been reduced to dried basil). Stir and cover.

Cook one pound spaghetti or fettuccine in boiling salted water until al dente. The way I tell if it's al dente is I hover over the pot, sampling a strand every 30 seconds or so. Be careful as for some reason it's hot. If the spaghetti is still too hard, throw it back in (as if freeing a fish). The boiling water will kill any of your germs.

Drain spaghetti water. Toss spaghetti and sauce in the same pot in which you cooked the spaghetti. Grate a fair amount of fresh Parmesan cheese (or, if necessary, pour from a canister of Kraft Parmesan-flavor woodpulp), grate more freshly ground pepper and serve, accompanied by ocean breeze or full-blast A/C or both.

Serves four.

GEORGE GARRETT

is the author of thirty-two books (poetry, fiction, plays, and non-fiction) and editor of nineteen others. He is Professor Emeritus at the University of Virginia. His latest book is *Southern Excursions,* a collection of essays on Southern literature.

Spaghetti Carbonara

(from George and Susan Garrett)

    This one goes back a while, almost fifty years in fact, to the days when we were living in Rome, back then when I was lean and mean and could pretty much eat what I pleased. (Anybody with cholesterol problems, stop reading now.) It's a traditional Roman dish, ostensibly created by the charcoal burners, hence its name. It wasn't much known in the States, back in those days, though the original and variations on it are fairly common now. Once in a while we still cook up a batch just for old times' sake and happy memories. Try it, you'll like it.

    This Roman dish is quick and easy to make. The hot spaghetti cooks the eggs.

About 6 ounces bacon (or Canadian bacon)
1 teaspoon olive oil
1 lb. spaghetti
4 eggs
Parmesan cheese
Black pepper
Chopped garlic (optional)

    Fry the bacon in a large pan until it is crisp. Drain and chop into small pieces. Pour off most of the fat and add a teaspoon of olive oil.

    Boil the spaghetti until it is al dente, not too soft. Drain and add to the frying pan.

    Beat the eggs slightly, add a quarter cup of the cheese, and right away mix vigorously with the hot spaghetti. Sprinkle with black pepper. Serve immediately, topped with more cheese, and chopped garlic if desired.

    Makes four servings.

BETH ANN FENNELLY

has published poems in many journals, including *The Kenyon Review* and *The American Scholar*. Her book *Open House* won the 2001 Kenyon Review Prize for a First Book and was nominated for an *L.A. Times* Book Award. She lives in Oxford, Mississippi.

Pesto: Why I Can't Cook for Your Self-Centered Cousin

The following poem of mine gives a great recipe for pesto. I usually eyeball the ingredients, but for those of you who are more precise, here are the complete measurements.

> 2 cups basil
> 3 cloves garlic
> ¼ cup pine nuts
> ¼ cup olive oil
> ½ cup Parmesan cheese
> ½ teaspoon salt

Why I Can't Cook for Your Self-Centered Architect Cousin

Because to me a dinner table's like a bed—
without love, it's all appetite and stains. Let's buy
take-out for your cousin, or order pizza—his toppings—

but I can't lift a spatula to serve him what I am.
Instead, invite our favorite misfits over: I'll feed
shaggy Otis who, after filet mignon, raised his plate

and sipped merlot sauce with such pleasure
my ego pardoned his manners. Or I'll call Mimi,
the chubby librarian, who paused over tiramisu—

"I haven't felt so satisfied since . . ." then cried
into its curls of chocolate. Or Randolph might stop by,
who once, celebrating his breakup with the vegetarian,

so packed the purse seine of his wiry body with shrimp
he unbuttoned his jeans and spent the evening
couched, "waiting for the swelling to go down."

Or maybe I'll just cook for us. I'll crush pine nuts
unhinged from the cone's prickly shingles.
I'll whittle the parmesan, and if I grate a knuckle

it's just more of me in my cooking. I'll disrobe
garlic cloves of rosy sheaths, thresh the basil
till moist, and liberate the oil. Then I'll dance

that green joy through the fettuccine, a tumbling,
leggy dish we'll imitate, after dessert.
If my embrace detects the five pounds you win

each year, you will merely seem a generous
portion. And if you bring my hand to your lips
and smell the garlic that lingers, that scents

the sweat you lick from the hollows of my clavicles,
you're tasting the reason I can't cook
for your cousin—my saucy, my strongly seasoned love.

HORTON FOOTE

has won two Academy Awards, the Pulitzer Prize for Drama, an Emmy Award, and two Writers Guild Awards. He is the author of over sixty plays and screenplays, including *To Kill a Mockingbird, Tender Mercies,* and *Tomorrow*. He has written two memoirs, *Farewell* and *Beginnings*.

Nan's Chicken Spaghetti

2 large chickens
2 ½ 12-ounce boxes of spaghetti
2 large onions, chopped
2 large bell peppers, chopped
7 or 8 stalks of celery, sliced
2 large cans of tomatoes
2 small cloves of garlic
½ lb. butter
2 or 3 bay leaves
1 large can of mushrooms, chopped
1 large can ripe olives, sliced
Salt and pepper to taste
Tabasco and Lea & Perrins to taste
Grated Parmesan cheese

Boil chicken in about 2 quarts water seasoned with salt. When tender, cool and cut into bite-size pieces and set aside. Save the water the chicken was boiled in. Saute onion, peppers, celery, and garlic in butter. Add seasonings and tomatoes and mushrooms. Simmer until done. Boil whole spaghetti, in the water the chicken was in, until done. Add tomato gravy mixture, chicken, and ripe olives. Cook together for a few minutes. Turn off heat and let steam, covered. Serve with Parmesan cheese sprinkled on top.

LILY TUCK

was born in Paris and lived in Thailand in the early 1960s. Her novel *Siam* was a finalist for the 2000 PEN/Faulkner Award. She also is the author of *Interviewing Matisse, The Woman Who Walked on Water,* and *Limbo and Other Places I Have Lived.* She lives in New York City.

700-Acre Island Spaghetti with Mussels

(with a nod to the River Café)

At dead low tide, my husband goes down to the beach with a bucket and brush to pick mussels. I tell him to pick the smallest ones—they are tenderer, I claim, than the bigger ones—and to pick about eight or ten mussels per person. Nonetheless he comes back with at least a hundred mussels in his bucket although we will only be four for dinner. (One of these days I will in fact tell him that we are going to be a hundred people for dinner and then we will see how many mussels he picks. . . . In any case our beach in Maine is covered with them.) Next my husband cleans the mussels. He runs them under cold water in the sink and pulls off the "beards," barnacles, and grit, discarding any open mussels. This takes quite a lot of time but he is meticulous about it. Meanwhile, I chop up 3 cloves of garlic, a handful of parsley, and set pans on the stove. When my husband is done, I boil up a half a cup of white wine and a few tablespoons of olive oil in my largest pot; once the oil and wine are boiling, we put in the mussels (easier than cooking lobsters, mussels don't make a sound). It does not take long; after the mussels have opened (we discard the mussels that stay shut), we drain them, careful to save the liquid. In another pan, I slowly brown the garlic and add a half a cup of heavy cream with about a teaspoon of chili powder; then I add the liquid (the wine and olive oil) in which we cooked the mussels and I cook this mixture until it is reduced by half. During this time the water for the spaghetti has come to a boil and I cook the spaghetti—a whole package for four people—and while the spaghetti is cooking and the cream is reducing, my husband and I are shelling the mussels as fast as we can (sometimes I find a little pearl). Once the cream sauce is reduced and the spaghetti is done, I drain it. The spaghetti goes in a pretty blue-and-green bowl my French friend, Francine, a potter, made, and I pour the cream sauce, to which, at the last minute, I have added the parsley. My husband adds the shelled mussels to the spaghetti, he has kept a few mussels in their shells for looks. We are ready to eat!

CURTIS WILKIE

is the author of *Dixie: A Personal Odyssey through Events That Shaped the Modern South.* He was a national and foreign correspondent for the *Boston Globe* for twenty-six years. He lives in Taylor, Mississippi, and New Orleans.

Pasta with Scallops
(and with apologies to whoever gave me this recipe)

Living in New Orleans, I cook in self-defense. If I tried to eat out every day in the city's endless collection of glorious restaurants, I'd either go broke or acquire the waistline of a sumo wrestler. During New Orleans' eleven-month summer, I grill a lot in my courtyard. (I highly recommend using a tin cone—Williams-Sonoma has them for about $12—with a wadded newspaper to fire the charcoal; the cones last for a couple of years and the method doesn't stink like the store-bought lighter fluid—$3 for about a half-dozen doses, and you risk singeing your eyebrows. But I digress.) Inside, in the kitchen, I tend to deal in pasta, since you can improvise with almost any kind of edible, converting the sorriest pieces of a whole chicken into a cacciatore that goes good with spaghetti or dumping leftover vegetables onto a bed of fettuccine and calling it "pasta primavera."

Here's one recipe that doesn't take too long once you've assembled the basic ingredients:

1 lb. linguine
1 lb. bay scallops
4 ounces safflower oil
2 red peppers
2 teaspoons lemon juice
½ cup toasted pine nuts
2 tablespoons chopped parsley
Salt and pepper to taste

A few words about the ingredients:
—Almost any kind of pasta will do other than angel-hair—too delicate for duty with this dish—or rigatoni—too bulky. When I lived in Jerusalem twenty years ago and consumer products were scarce, I made my own pasta. But making pasta is as big a pain in the butt as tending to magnolia trees, so I find it simpler to buy a package of dry pasta.

—The scallops must be fresh, if you can't find bay scallops, use sea scallops and cut them into dice-size portions before cooking.

—I find that safflower sears scallops better, but if you don't have any, use plain old virgin olive oil.

—The peppers must be roasted ahead of time. When I'm cooking out I throw them on a grill until charred black, then cover them in a pot until cool enough for me to peel away the blacked skin, core and remove the seeds and cut the tasty remains into julienne strips. The *peperone arrosti,* as the Italians call it, can be stored for several days in a covered container in the refrigerator.

—Pine nuts can be toasted to a golden brown in a couple of minutes, but don't forget or they'll be cinders in another two minutes.

—Fresh parsley looks better, but dried parsley is acceptable.

While the pasta water is boiling, heat half of the oil in a heavy skillet and sear the scallops—a handful at a time, turning them golden on all sides before transferring to a bowl (takes no more than a couple of minutes for each batch). When finished with scallops, pour remainder of oil, lemon juice, roasted peppers, and parsley into the skillet just long enough to heat these ingredients, then move them into the bowl with scallops. This should be timed to coincide with the completion of the cooked pasta. Drain the pasta and mix it into a big bowl with the aforementioned ingredients, throw in the pine nuts (toasted while the scallops are searing), add salt and pepper and toss.

Cooking time: 20 minutes max.

Serves four, sometimes more. Leftovers can be reheated.

Enjoy.

ROBERT O'CONNOR

was chosen by Granta as one of the Best of Young American Novelists. He teaches English and creative writing at the State University of New York at Oswego. He is the author of *Buffalo Soldiers.*

I Left My Hearts under the Volcano Pasta

Cooking, when it's going well, is like writing; immense care and precision taken by one person for the pleasure of many. When I cooked this recipe, I lived alone and in reduced circumstances and cooked only for myself.

- 1 lb. turkey hearts (Do not attempt to collect individually. Very messy and inconvenient to the turkeys.)
- 1 lb. pasta (Your choice. I prefer rotini. They remind me of corkscrews and wine without screwtops.)
- 1 jar Aunt Millie's Tomato Sauce (I don't think she's a real person.)

1. Boil water for the macaroni. Add salt to raise the temperature.
2. Dump in pasta and cook until it's soft. Stir occasionally, particularly when it's about to boil over.
3. Pour Aunt Millie's sauce into saucepan. Light low flame. Stir occasionally and be alert for that burning smell.
4. Oh, the turkey hearts. This is the tricky part. Put them in a plastic bowl. Cover with new Saran Wrap that has enough tensile strength to be used recovering old couches.
5. Cook the turkey hearts for 10 minutes on Hi in the microwave. When the turkey hearts explode like little grenades, don't think of it as yet another defeat and get down on your life, but rather as a shortcut in the eating process. (You no longer have to slice your meat, just scrape it off the interior of the microwave. If you used the proper Saran Wrap, this will take less time.)

WARNING: This is not for the faint of hearts.

TONY EARLEY

is the author of *Somehow Form a Family*, *Jim the Boy*, and *Here We Are in Paradise: Stories*. He was chosen for Granta's Best of Young American Novelists and was awarded a National Magazine Award for Fiction.

Liar's Linguine

4 cored, sliced, then quartered tomatoes
4 fat cloves of garlic
½ cup walnuts, chopped
½ cup or so fresh basil, chopped
1 yellow bell pepper, cut in strips
1 red bell pepper, cut in strips
1 or 2 tablespoons olive oil (use to taste)
Salt
Pepper
½ seedless orange, sectioned
1 big box linguine

Assemble and prepare ingredients before guests arrive. Arrange ingredients on wooden cutting board, leave in plain view.

Invite guests into kitchen while you cook, the closer to the stove the better. Heat olive oil, medium heat, in large, Teflon-coated skillet. Press garlic into olive oil. Open garlic press, remove pulp, throw into skillet, too. Tell guests how when you were a little boy you almost stepped on a copperhead in the forest. Tell them how you looked around until you found a large stick with which to kill snake; how when you hit snake with stick, stick broke, snake jumped and landed on broken end of stick; how on backswing for second whack at snake, you threw snake straight up into the air. Stir garlic with wooden spoon. Wait until eyebrows of guests go up. Say, "And to this day I don't know where that snake came down."

Add yellow and red pepper strips; stir until beautiful. Tell them about Larry, the guy from Racine, Wisconsin, you knew in college. Tell them Larry's nickname was "the Midwesterner," that he was the most deliberate guy you ever saw, how he used to win the dorm ping-pong tournaments simply by hitting everything back, no slams, no spin, no nothing, just hitting it back, yup, yup, yo. Tell them how the night North Carolina defeated Georgetown for the NCAA basketball championship you and Larry had to be separated because Larry said Carolina was lucky. Tell them how Larry was allergic to nuts, how he said if he ever ate a nut it would kill him, how he went down the cafeteria line pointing and saying, "That got nuts in it? That got nuts in it?" Add walnuts.

Stir. Maybe turn down heat. Tell them how Larry had a crush on Cherry, a beautiful girl from a strict, Baptist family. (Do not tell them that her name was really Sherry; remember all measurements need only be approximate.) Tell them how Larry never told Cherry how he felt because he was too shy. Tell them how Cherry had never been away from her parents before, how in the student union you saw her take her first sip of wine, how you saw her dance for the first time. Tell them how Cherry was the most sexually suggestive dancer you ever saw, how she danced like Salome, or Fatima of the seven veils, how Larry stood in the corner and watched for hours, and how when you mentioned to her that she was a very sexual dancer she grew angry, blushed, said, "What do you mean?" and stormed away. Put linguine in big pot of boiling water. Tell them how Cherry quit school and married the first guy who ever asked her out on a date. Tell them that the last you heard Larry was managing a men's department in a Wisconsin Sears. Tell them how you never asked Cherry out because you had grown up Baptist, too, that you had just left your parents for the first time, that Cherry saw you take your first sip of wine. Tell them how you were holding out for an Episcopalian, wink at wife.

Turn down heat. Add basil. Add tomatoes. Add orange sections. Tell guests that living in a rusting steel town down the river from Pittsburgh isn't so bad, although it took some getting used to. Tell them how at a community dinner at the Greek Orthodox church you fell in love with the lemon potatoes. Tell them how you had to have the recipe, how you wanted those potatoes to be part of your life, how you walked up to the old woman serving the potatoes and said, "Hey, how did y'all fix those potatoes?" Tell them how the woman's eyes grew wide, how she looked first to the old woman on one side of her, and then to the old woman on the other, leaned over the counter toward you and said, a little more harshly than you might have hoped, "We *cooked* 'em." Drain linguine. Tell them how on the way home from the Greek Orthodox church, in the middle of this town where the houses are so close together that you can lean out the window of one and knock on the window of the one across the alley, that you saw a deer, a beautiful doe, cross the street in front of your car and disappear into a small, brushy ravine. Tell them how you were so surprised, so suddenly homesick for North Carolina, that you stopped your car and waited, hoping the deer would reappear. Wait until you see your guests smile, stare into space. Say, "Of course, it *was* smoking a cigarette." Salt and pepper to taste. Spoon over linguine. Serve hot.

Tony Earley

JONATHAN FRANZEN

is a frequent contributor to the *New Yorker* and *Harper's*. He won the 2001 National Book Award for his novel *The Corrections*. He also wrote *How to Be Alone: Essays, Strong Motion,* and *The Twenty-Seventh City*. He lives in New York.

Pasta with Kale

This is good food for a working writer: cheap, easy to make, handsome, elegant, nutritionally well-balanced, devoid of saturated fat, private, erotic, virtuous, delicious. I eat it hot the first night and then cold as leftovers for two further dinners and maybe one lunch.

    1 lb. fresh kale
    1 lb. good dry pasta, ideally Del Verde brand
    1 kettle of water with lots of salt
    3 medium-size garlic cloves
    ½ cup (or less) extra-virgin olive oil
    Salt and pepper to taste

Boil water in a kettle. Peel the garlic and chop it up. Wash the kale, tearing it into pieces roughly the size of playing cards (throw away the lower, woodier two-thirds of the stems), and pile it into a pot. Add a little water, if necessary, to make maybe a quarter-inch on the bottom of the pot. Cover with a lid. Sauté the garlic (and some salt) in the olive oil until the garlic just barely begins to brown; remove from heat. Add pasta to the boiling water and stir it a little. Turn on high heat under the kale and steam/boil it, tossing it once or twice, until it's fully wilted; pour off any excess liquid. When the pasta is al dente, drain it and toss it with the kale, garlic, and oil. Some pepper may be ground over it. Grated cheese, however, is a desecration.

BEBE MOORE CAMPBELL

is the author of *Singing in the Comeback Choir, Sweet Summer, Growing up with and without My Dad, Your Blues Ain't Like Mine,* and *Brothers and Sisters.*

Fast Pasta

People say I'm a good cook. Truth is, I don't cook all that often, maybe two or three times a week (not like my grandmother, who cooked a fresh meal every night, but much better than my mother, who doesn't cook at all). I hate routine cooking. What I look for in deciding to prepare a meal during the week is something fast that can be done up in one pot. This dish calls for two (one for boiling the pasta), but the saving grace is that after I dump the rigatoni in with the sauce, I only have to wash one pot that night, because I store what's left in the same pot. This minor detail is extremely important to me.

You need one package of ground turkey; smoked turkey sausage; chopped onion; minced garlic; about half a jar of Ragu spaghetti sauce, the kind with mushrooms and peppers (Shortcuts are a good thing.); basil; pepper; season salt; garlic powder; some white wine; olive oil; half a can of peeled tomatoes; half a jar of sun dried tomatoes in olive oil.

Season the onions and garlic and saute them in olive oil on a medium high flame in an iron skillet. (I used to be anemic, so I cook everything in an iron pot.) Chop up the turkey sausage and throw that in. Add the ground turkey. Season everything again and let it brown. Add the sun dried tomatoes with a little of the olive oil. Add the canned tomatoes and some of the juice. Mix the white wine and Ragu together and dump that in. Cover the pot. Turn down the heat and let it simmer. Boil the rigatoni or penne pasta. Throw the pasta into the sauce. Dig in!

Bebe Moore Campbell

ROBERT O'CONNOR

Biographical statement, p. 53.

The Oliver Twist Omelette

When you're happy with your writing and life, use this recipe.

    3 eggs, extra large or jumbo
    1 slice of Swiss cheese about the size of a legal envelope
    2 slices American cheese
    Barbecue sauce
    1 child of appropriate age (5 or under)

1. Beat eggs into a fine froth.
2. Grease your frying pan with butter. (It's important in these troubled times to live dangerously. If you've already given up smoking, that's enough virtue for one person. If you've never smoked, add an extra slice of American cheese to the ingredients, or eat it while making the omelette.)
3. Pour whipped eggs into pan. Watch with satisfaction as the lunar landscape appears.
4. Cover one-half of the omelette with Swiss cheese and place the 2 American slices on top. You may tear them into smaller pieces to get good consistency.
5. Pour barbecue sauce to taste. Note: It is important here to show restraint. Like adjectives and adverbs, you only need a little to make your point, and too much will cause your stomach lining to erode. Restraint is a good thing to develop in any case.
6. Before the cheese has melted completely, flip the unpaved portion of the omelette over. Once that cooks, flip the whole omelette. After the second flip, be sure to use your spatula to press down on the omelette to squeeze some cheese and barbecue sauce onto the pan, where it will burn to a light, delicious edge.
7. Slide it onto a plate. Don't worry if it's messy. This is art we're talking.
8. Take two forks, one for you, and one for your child. I use my son, Jackson, now three. Place him in the chair next to you. If he's a mouth-breather and lip-smacker, it's important to have a little distance.
9. Jackson will say, "Can I have some?" You will cut pieces of the egg for him, avoiding the barbecue sections, as that is a vice that must be learned later in life.

10. Feed him with one hand, yourself with the other. Do not neglect his cries of "Can I have some?" by shoveling food first into your own mouth, because there are few enough chances in this life to show love, and they should be seized and held as long as possible. You will remember this moment forever, although he will soon forget it, and what you will remember is the light in his eyes as the food touches his lips, made all the sweeter by your knowledge that this moment, like food, like love, like writing, like life, will never be repeated exactly the same way.

MILLER WILLIAMS

is a poet and teacher in Fayetteville, Arkansas, and author of thirty-one books, including fifteen collections of poetry. His awards include the Prix de Rome for Literature, the Academy Award for Literature, and the Poet's Prize.

Eggs Arkansas

The Night Before:

Being an Arkie from the hills, I know that the most important thing is the proper attire for an occasion. If it's just us, I choose my most debonair pj's; if we have company, I pick out some more casual clothes, but if my brother from California is here I get down into the bottom of my closet for a pair of madras shorts that I almost never wear.

Then I fix myself a glass of bourbon and branch water so that I can relax into the proper sleep to be ready for the Sunday morning occasion.

Sunday Morning:

Having prepared coffee the night before (which I should have mentioned) I turn the pot on and begin to make the Bloody Marys (though mimosas will do as well). Being the chef, I always make a Virgin Mary for myself. As my wife sets the table, I begin to prepare the Eggs Arkansas. Here's the recipe.

While an egg is poaching and a sausage patty frying for each serving (many will want two), warm in a horizontal toaster for each serving half an English muffin topped with a slice of Monterey Jack cheese. When the muffins are ready, add to each a sausage patty and a poached egg on that, then top it off with a good dose of warm picante sauce. Serve it at once—with strong coffee (at my house, anyway).

Enjoy.

ELI EVANS

is the author of *The Provincials: A Personal History of Jews in the South, The Lonely Days Were Sundays: Reflections of a Jewish Southerner,* and *Judah P. Benjamin: The Jewish Confederate.* A North Carolina native, he lives with his wife and son in New York City, where he is president of the Charles H. Revson Foundation.

Eli's Kosher Grits

(Excerpted from *The Provincials: A Personal History of Jews in the South.*)

After *The Provincials* was published in 1973, I received a phone call asking me to enter a contest that Quaker Oats was running to promote a new line of quick grits.

You can imagine my astonishment when my entry was selected as a contest finalist. I suspected, when it came to grits, my gimmick had caught the judges' eye and an Atlanta-originated idea must have fit the bill.

All the finalists were invited to an evening at Tavern on the Green to mill around with the judges for the competition—such Southern celebrities as Tommy Tune and Lynda Bird Johnson from Texas, Tom Wolfe from Virginia (before he wrote *The Right Stuff* and *Bonfire of the Vanities*), and Craig Claiborne from Mississippi (food critic for the *New York Times*). They would spend the evening sampling the huge selection of grits exotica and, as a finale, declare the winners. We cocky competitors wandered around with a gleam in our eye because we all knew, blue ribbon or not, we would each be receiving the equivalent of an Academy Award in this field—a year's supply of grits. It was one of those crazy New York events, packed with every Southerner in town, dressed to the nines and sipping champagne to wash down the evening's unassuming fare as if it were caviar. Meanwhile, the dark-suited Quaker Oats officials jabbered into walkie-talkies and scurried around taking themselves and this competition very seriously indeed. The center of attention was the fabulous array of grits concoctions beautifully arranged on a long table featuring silver platters, white linen tablecloths, and candelabra. Bustling butlers served with elan, as if to disguise for the evening the humble origins of the regional delicacy we were celebrating.

It was a grits festival in the Big Apple with background melodies like "Autumn in New York" and "I'll Take Manhattan" played by a Juilliard Quartet. Here and there and everywhere were grits puttin' on the ritz. Gourmet grits with brie and toasted almonds elegantly shared the long tables with trendy, health-conscious grits with asparagus and sprigs of watercress; there lay Mexican grits with black beans and guacamole; even dessert grits with all manner of fruits and flambées and sauces. And then, as a reminder of its versatility, there was a mound of unadorned plain lifeless grits, lying inert (as grits are wont to do), ready for the topping of your choice, when it would turn into a plain ingenue in a party dress. Grits amidst the glitz.

But, boy, was I proud to see Eli's Kosher Grits out there on the bedazzled groaning board, with a lightbulb beside the china to dramatize the secret of the recipe. I watched with an air of nervous nonchalance as the distinguished judges tasted it and harrumphed among themselves. Finally, in a white tuxedo, Tommy Tune, the 6-foot, 10-inch tap dancer, rat-a-tat-tatted over to the table, and all eyes were riveted as he spooned my masterpiece all the way up to his mouth (no short trip), savored (without expression) a sizable spoonful, and declared as if he wore black robes: "Cute idea—but ordinary, really."

Oh well. It's still the closest I've ever been to becoming immortal, to getting to eat lunch with James Beard, or to trading recipes with Julia Child. So, y'all, here is the prize-eluding recipe, 100% guaranteed to release hidden memories of childhood if consumed before an oral history interview.

Put Quaker Oats Instant Grits into boiling salted water and stir over low heat until firm. Then take an old light bulb, and push the large end into the grits to make an indentation. Break one or two eggs into the impression, then cover so the eggs poach gently in the steaming grits. Sprinkle with crisp crumpled bits of sauteed (or fried, as they say Down South) pastrami (that's the kosher part) or buttered rye-toast croutons. Add salt and pepper to taste. Remove from the heat and spoon into a bowl. Enjoy. A 10-inch skillet will accommodate six eggs. The light bulb detail adds character to the undertaking. (But, frankly, it won't get you into *Gourmet* magazine.) By the way, since everyone at the contest wanted to know, a 40-watt bulb does fine for one egg.

Eli N. Evans

ELMORE LEONARD

was born in New Orleans and has been "confined to the Detroit area since 1935." He has written thirty-seven novels, including *When the Women Come Out to Dance, Get Shorty, Freaky Deaky,* and *Tishomingo Blues,* seventeen of which have been made into movies.

Elmore's Southron Breakfast Treats

Put two packets of Quaker Minute Grits in a bowl, pour in a cup of boiling water, stir, add a pat of butter, salt to taste, and eat it. Mmmmm. Now open a can of Underwood Deviled Ham—the one with the red devil on the white wrapper. Spread it on a slice of bread of your choice. Next, chop up a stalk of celery and sprinkle it all over the Deviled Ham. Top it off with another slice of bread and you have a delicious sandwich to start your day.

Other nourishing starters are cheese and jelly sandwiches and cold bean sandwiches with chopped onions. If you're over seventy you might want to have a glass of prune juice first. Have a nice day.

FANNIE FLAGG

is the author of *Daisy Fay and the Miracle Man, Welcome to the World, Baby Girl!* and, most recently, *Standing in the Rainbow.* Her script for the film adaption of her novel *Fried Green Tomatoes at the Whistle Stop Café* was nominated for an Academy Award. She lives in California and Alabama.

Grits

The Whistle Stop Café opened up last week. . . . If there is anybody that has not been there yet, Idgie says that the breakfast hours are from 5:30 to 7:30, and you can get eggs, grits, biscuits, bacon, sausage, ham and red-eye gravy, and coffee for 25 cents.

(from *Fried Green Tomatoes at the Whistle Stop Café*, reprinted with the author's permission)

2 tablespoons butter
1 teaspoon salt
5 cups boiling water
1 cup hominy grits

Add lots of butter and salt to the boiling water. Slowly stir in the grits. Cover and cook slowly for about 30 to 40 minutes, and stir till you like it.

Keeps you regular.

Fannie Flagg

STEWS, SOUPS &
A LOT OF CHILI

You have obviously never tasted my cooking
or I would have been eliminated early.

— LEWIS NORDAN

JIM HARRISON

is a poet and novelist. He has held a National Endowment for the Arts grant and a Guggenheim Fellowship. He is the author of *Legends of the Fall, Just before Dark, The Beast God Forgot to Invent, Dalva,* and *Off to the Side,* a memoir.

Posole from Sonora

I can't write out recipes they're impossible. Life is not a list. A recipe is always a circle which one, however ineptly, dances around. I was recently at a literary party in Aix-en-Provence and at their local open market there was enough to keep me busy for months. Hundreds of kinds of vegetables, fifty kinds of olives, fifty different kinds of fish, fresh herbs, rabbits, quails, ducks, veal, etc.

It takes a great deal of wit to cook in America and the ample use of Federal Express unless one lives in New York, San Francisco, or Seattle. I get my wine from Kermit Lynch Importers in Berkley, California. It's unthinkable to cook without drinking wine while doing so, in fact my motto is, "Drink wine or someone will drink it in your place." For instance, I can't make the following recipe called posole from Sonora without using ingredients I get from Gary Nabham at the Native Seed Search, 2509 N. Campbell Avenue, Tucson, AZ 85710 (602-327-9123). Dried posole or hominy is much better than the canned variety though you can use the canned variety. Simmer a shoulder roast of pork until it begins to delaminate. If you have dried posole you cook it along with it. If canned add 2 cans at the end. Put in ½ cup of chopped garlic and ½ cup of either fresh or tinned jalapenos. I won't make this dish unless I have *chimayo* ground chiles which can be purchased from the above address. You serve this with chopped radishes, onions, and tortillas. When I am on the border I add a calves foot to silken the juices, but a couple of small pigs feet will do. This is a generic Sonoran stew and I've made it with bear, lamb shanks, an elk neck, or antelope shanks. Pork is fine though. It's better if you can get local pork that hasn't suffered a monochromatic diet. I could also add "salt to taste," but I am assuming that. Chopped fresh cilantro is a nice addition while cooking it and at serving, if you can get it.

Jim Harrison

TOM FRANKLIN

is the author of *Poachers,* a collection of stories, and *Hell at the Breech,* a novel. The recipient of a Guggenheim Fellowship and an Arkansas Arts Council Grant, Franklin also was a Tennessee Williams Fellow at the University of the South in Sewanee, Tennessee.

Chubb Stew

Note: Embarrassing as it is, my wife's nickname for me is "Chubby" or "Chubb" (see page 47). The following recipe is part of the reason why I've gained a few pounds over the last couple of years.

Begin with the meat.

When I buy meat for a Chubb stew, I usually select a hearty rump roast; I like the heft of it in my hand, a good solid hunk of meat. I might pay 6 or 8 bucks for it, but the benefits are as follows: I can cut it up into the larger chunks I like in my stews; I can leave any excess fat on the counter; and, with my roast being a better cut of meat than is often used for stewing, the ultimate taste/texture is—in my opinion—better. You can also use venison when it's available, lamb, or any other good stewing meat. Or any combination. The more meat, the better.

When my Frugal Wife buys the meat for Chubb stew, however, she invariably selects a package of precut chunks called "stewing meat," which is usually only a couple of bucks. I don't like the concept of stewing meat because it's almost always the cheapest, lousiest throw-away cuts, and it's often fattier than I like. When it comes to meat, I like to be involved. To cut it myself. To decide how much fat is left on. The obvious advantage of stewing meat is, of course, that you don't have to cut it up, but still, often I find myself sawing off fat and wishing I'd gone to the store myself and gotten the above-mentioned rump roast: if I'm going to be hacking at the meat, I'd prefer it on my own terms. Man, knife, big-ass slab of meat.

To prepare your meat once it's cut into pieces, dust it with a combination of flour, garlic salt, and pepper, then throw it into a skillet and brown it; this will aid in giving you a classier gravy.

Which is a good transition to broth.

Start, of course, with beer. I prefer Bud Light, but I suppose Miller or Pabst Blue Ribbon will work fine. Avoid Keystone. What's best is a green beer—in other words a beer some jerk at a party took from the cooler and left unopened but sitting out so that it got warm. Where I used to throw these away or re-cool and then force them down, I now put them in my special Chubb stew cabinet.

(Important note: one can of beer is enough. Once, in the early days of developing the recipe for Chubb stew and of the mind that if one beer is good, six must be better, I used a whole six pack. This batch of Chubb stew did not taste good. My Frugal Wife, aware that I'd wasted five beers, pointed out that you only need one for flavoring.)

Now. Put your floured, browned meat into a large pot on high heat and pour the can of beer over it. This won't be enough liquid to cover your hearty chunks of meat, so you must add more stuff. I recommend whatever coffee is left in the coffee pot from the morning. Trust me on this. A little red wine's good, too, even a half-finished can of warm Dr. Pepper. (Or, of course, any combination.) And a bit of soy sauce and some Worcestershire. For the rest, use tap water until the meat is fully covered.

Your Frugal Wife will agree with you here. You're using up things, old coffee, half cans of soda, ruined beer. Make sure that when you add these ingredients, your Frugal Wife sees you.

Meanwhile, keep a close eye on your stew, and don't let the liquid level fall below the meat.

Now put a couple of beef or chicken bullion cubes into the mix, using a wooden spoon to crush them. Toss in a few bay leaves while you're at it. (My Frugal Wife says 2 or 3, I say 4 or 5.) And sprinkle in the following spices, to taste: chili pepper, cayenne pepper, more garlic salt, regular salt, black pepper, basil, oregano, and hot sauce. If you like your broth extra thick, you can add in the rest of the floury mix you used to dust the meat. And if you like it *really* thick, add in a packet of brown gravy mix.

By now you've got a good seething pot going. I like to let this stew for 2 or 3 hours, stirring it occasionally, making sure nothing sticks to the bottom. At this point, the meat's getting good and tender. Sample a few pieces. Drink a cold Bud Light. Add more spices to taste, usually when your Frugal Wife is out watering her garden or doing yoga. Turn the heat down and let the simmering begin.

And now the vegetables. The ones you use may vary, but here are what I consider staples: unpeeled potatoes, white onions, carrots, celery, and green peppers. Cut these up into the sizes and shapes that please you and add them in whenever you'd like. The amount is left up to you. I like carrots and onions the best, so my Chubb stews are heavy on these.

I like to buy a bag of already-cut, already-cleaned carrots because I hate peeling carrots. Sure, the bags are more expensive and, sure, your Frugal Wife would prefer you to save the money, but often there's a baseball game on shortly and those carrot-peeling devices are hard to master.

As for onions, I can't find a way around the eye-burning except to wear wood-cutting goggles. One ploy is as follows: lure your Frugal Wife into the kitchen with a glass of red wine. Put Her Music on the CD player. Sade. Tori Amos. Opera. Whatever. While you pretend to be having difficulty with some other aspect of the stew, she'll notice the strategically placed cutting board, knife, and onions on the counter. Without even thinking, she'll begin cutting. You're halfway across the kitchen, out of the Burn Zone. (Note: this ploy also works with the cutting of other vegetables.)

For myself, I like vegetables very tender, almost-falling-apart tender, so I add the potatoes and onions after the meat's been cooking only an hour or so. The rest can go in an hour or two later. If you like your celery and carrots crunchier, wait to add them until an hour before you take the stew off.

Now it's time to let it cook. I say the longer the better—a whole day of simmering is perfect, though 4 or 5 hours will be fine. If you're lucky there's a Braves game on and Maddux is pitching. Or Glavine. If you're really lucky, they win. Soon, you'll be able to settle down to eat on your Chubb stew for several days. You'll find it works for any meal, too—though it's best with coffee or Dr. Pepper at breakfast, Bud Light at lunch, and red wine at dinner.

ROBERT LOVE TAYLOR

Biographical statement, p. 35.

My Stepfather Jimmy's Recipe for Beef Stew

(transcribed by Robert Love Taylor)

    2 lbs. of meat
    2 large potatoes
    2 onions, medium size
    1 rutabaga
    2 cans of stewed tomatoes "Mex"
    4 small carrots
    1 green pepper
    3 stalks of celery
    1 can beef consommé
    1 tablespoon of wheat germ
    2 cloves of garlic, minced
    1 small can of cut green beans

Cut meat into small cubes. Chop one onion. Saute for about 10 to 20 minutes in 1 tablespoon of oil or butter or whatever you have.

Have all of your vegetables ready to go. Small cubes in the pot: carrots, onions, rutabaga. While sauteing, add the following spices:

    1 tablespoon of chili powder
    ½ teaspoon ginger—after
    thyme
    allspice
    onion powder
    garlic powder
    nutmeg
    mint
    1 tablespoon Perrins
    1 teaspoon liquid smoke
    1 tablespoon A-1 sauce

After the sauteing, put in the consommé and all the rest with 1 ½ cans of water and 2 bay leaves. Use your own judgment on the salt and pepper and red pepper. Most times I start with some for sauteing, then add more as I go along.

Bring to boil. Return to simmer or low boil for about 45 minutes to 1 hour. Stir about every 10 minutes.

If the stew is too thin, thicken with instant potatoes or cornstarch. If you have to use flour or cornstarch, mix it in a glass a little at a time or it will be lumpy. Use lean beef and the best you can afford. I use sirloin tips.

You have to remember about the condiments: you can put them in, but you can't take them out. So I would use only about half as much until it suits your taste.

Your basic stew: meat, potatoes, celery, carrots, onions, spices. You don't have to put in the rest of it unless you want it. But remember it's a stew you're making, not a soup.

Jimmy

PADGETT POWELL

is the author of *A Woman Named Drown, Aliens of Affection, Typical,* and *Mrs. Hollingworth's Men,* which was nominated for the National Book Award. He lives in Gainesville, Florida.

Cur Gumbo Full of Choices and Options

The first time I saw gumbo made it was made by Barry Ancelet, the dean of things Cajun, and I was hooked—by the mystery and beauty of stopping the roux with the cold vegetables. That pinned me wriggling to the kitchen wall. Consequently, though I have read many recipes and am aware of sophistications and subtleties in gumbo and in gumbo cooking, for me the beauty of it is less in the eating than in that searing, violent, gentle collision and wedding of the cooked and the raw.

Get a Magnalite pot (oval roaster is good), a shiny one, not the brushed commercial stuff, by calling General Housewares Corp., 1-800-545-4411. You have to have this cookware if you want to do it right. You could use iron or Le Creuset, but you'd be more of a fraud than following this outlander recipe of mine is already going to make of you.

Chop your vegetables. The "trinity" is celery, onions, and bell peppers, in arcanely varying proportions (cf. Prudhomme), but I profanate with heavy parsley, other sweet and hot peppers, and green onions. I clean out the vegetable bin, which is what gumbo is good for. The roux stopping essentially disintegrates the vegetables anyway.

2 cups onions	*These are chopped and ready, like soldiers on the edge of a battle. Use any troops you have, in any combination.*
2 cups celery	
2 cups bell pepper	
1 cup other peppers	
1 cup parsley	
1 cup green onions	

For meat, what's on hand is about what goes in. There are verboten combinations but I can't learn them. Use some meat—let's use chicken and sausage, a standard. Whatever you use, match the stock to it, within reason (turf to turf, sea to sea).

Season 2 cups of flour with whatever you like to season flour with—salt, pepper, paprika, garlic powder, and cinnamon are good for chicken; delete cinnamon, add sage for pork, perhaps. This seasoning is the second zone of your personalizing options, of which modern life is so godforsakenly rich. The first zone of CHOICES was above in the vegetables.

Dredge chicken in the flour, brown it and your sausage in the Magnalite in oil sufficient to cover the bottom of the pan well, say a quarter inch. Oil in gumbo cooking is also an arcane science; there are long disquisitions on which oils to use in what ratio, and on how they will separate later if something happens, or does not happen, and what you do, or don't do, then. Prudhomme famously mixes lard and oil and butter, and tons of it. Just use olive oil.

Brown the meat—just brown it. You want the meat to be rare even in the finished dish if you can manage it. Leave seafood raw. Remove browned meat and add seasoned flour to the oil, now somewhat less than a quarter inch, and the browning residues—again, cover the bottom of pan. As near as I can tell, the oil and flour bind together in a 1:1 (volume) ratio; just dust the flour in until it looks like you'll have a roux about as heavy as syrup (too loose and some oil will not bind up; too stiff and the roux won't level well and will be impossible to cook through). Make a dark roux (that is to say, toast your flour in this oil.) Prudhomme says a light roux for dark meat, a dark for light; I think a dark roux is always better. I know nothing.

I heat roux much more slowly than books say, and thereby avoid burning it, about which you can also read aplenty. Take it slowly, stirring, scraping (I use a good metal spatula for all phases of roux making)—occasionally check your soldiers and take a whiff of their new-mown-grassy greenness—until roux is deep brown. When you see smoke or smell toast, or when you can't stand it, dump in vegetables and cut the heat.

Stir. The vegetables are, I believe, sublimated, and the kitchen is, for the nonce, a sublime place. All present are seduced. Women inclined to say No will say Yes. The house itself is in a swoon. You can stop right here; actually eating the gumbo can be de trop to this moment. But we are Christians, even if we aren't, and must slog on.

In the Magnalite, once shiny and proud, will be a tarry goo with what looks like molten jujubes in it. People who know what they are talking about will tell you to spoon this mixture slowly into your hot stock, so that the flour blooms, or whatever flour does when you make gravy, which is essentially what you are trying to make, a big broad gravy. But I say just pour in your stock (4 to 6 cups), even cold, and heat the whole thing up.

Finishing the gumbo, now, is no more than soup making, but there are special gumbo rules, which I choose, exercising another cloying choice, to ignore. Tomatoes are contraindicated some of the time, as is okra, and you don't put certain things together—God. Add tomatoes (a large can, or half dozen fresh) if you are adding them, okra ditto (several cups, frozen, fresh, baby whole or chopped—choices), correct seasoning, and just before serving add the meat or seafood. Serve over not-gummed-up rice, or neat in the morning (a hangover food to rival menudo). Add filé at the table—if you like it. I find it redundant to the okra, and maybe it is added only in the absence of okra and we have another index of my ignorance of gumbo propriety—and fresh, chopped green onions.

RICK CLEVELAND

has been a sportswriter for the *Clarion-Ledger* in Jackson, Mississippi, for thirty years. He is the author of *It's More Than a Game* and *Vaught: The Man and His Legacy*.

Killer Gumbo Ya-Ya That Won't Kill You

Stock

Do this the day before to allow the stock to sit in refrigerator overnight, which will make defatting the stock easy. Two smoked chickens (smoke 'em yourself or buy 'em already smoked). Water to cover. One onion, celery tops, and several cloves of garlic. Put whole chickens in stock pot with onion, celery, and garlic, cover with water and bring to a boil. Immediately reduce heat to low and let simmer 2 to 3 hours. Remove chicken and strain stock through a fine colander and put liquid in refrigerator overnight. Fat will rise to surface and solidify for easy removal. Debone chicken and, using fingers, break into pieces (size won't matter because it will fall apart in gumbo anyway) and put in refrigerator.

Other Ingredients

    2 lbs. Andouille sausage (or another meaty smoked sausage), diced into ½ inch cubes
       (this can be blanched to reduce fat)
    2 large onions, chopped
    2 green bell peppers, chopped
    5 stalks celery, chopped
    5 cloves garlic, finely chopped
    1 ½ pounds okra, sliced ¼ inch thick
    1 bunch of mustard or turnip greens (or 1 bag pre-cleaned and pre-cut), chopped
    1 ½ cup 100% apple juice
    1 cup of browned flour or instant dry roux mix like Cacheres or Zatarans (to make
       your own, put flour in dry baking dish and bake in a 350° oven until brown—times
       vary broadly in different ovens)

Seasoning Mix (mixed in advance)

    1 ½ tablespoons sea salt
    2 tablespoons dry mustard
    2 tablespoons paprika
    2 tablespoons onion powder

1 ½ tablespoons garlic powder

1 ½ tablespoons dried basil

1 tablespoon dried thyme

1 tablespoon dried oregano

2 teaspoons black pepper

2 teaspoons white pepper

1 or 2 teaspoons or more cayenne pepper (make as hot as you like, but remember you can perk it up at the table but not down)

Preparations

In stock pot, bring smoked chicken stock to boil. In another large—or gumbo—pot, preferably non-stick (if you use a regular pot, use some non-stick spray on bottom) over medium high heat, cook the onions, bell peppers, and celery, stirring often, for 3 minutes. Add half the greens and half the okra and cook 2 more minutes, stirring to check for sticking. Add the apple juice and cook until most of the liquid is gone, probably about 6 to 7 minutes. Add the browned flour or roux mix and half the seasoning mix and begin stirring as it cooks. Cook until the graininess of the flour disappears and a smooth paste forms (if the flour is sticking, add half a ladle of the hot stock to help break it up). Add the sausage, chicken, half the remaining seasoning mix, and all of the remaining vegetables and reduce heat to medium and continue to stir. This will build muscles because it can be thick. Cook 5 to 8 minutes. Then begin adding the boiling stock, about a cup at a time, stirring until it is well mixed before adding another cup. Keep adding the stock until desired thickness is achieved. Do not overdo the stock because you can always thin it with more stock. Bring to a boil, and reduce heat to a simmer and allow one hour for all flavors to marry, stirring often to make sure bottom of the pot is not sticking (if it begins to stick and scorch, do not scrape the bottom, just remove the gumbo to another pot immediately. Taste and adjust seasoning (you have ¼ of the seasoning mix left). Serve over rice and eat plenty. Stir the pot well during serving, because this lite gumbo has a tendency to separate a little. This is a healthy gumbo. My brother Bobby hasn't had another heart attack since he started eating it. (See page 114.) Use any leftover stock for other recipes or freeze it in an ice-cube tray to use as needed.

HOWARD NORMAN

is the author of the novels *The Northern Lights, The Bird Artist, The Haunting of L.*, and *Amorous Window*. He teaches English at the University of Maryland.

The Julianne Ortale Three-Sausage Spicy Jambalaya for Lake Boat, Picnic or Kitchen Table

9 chicken thighs, or 4 thighs and 5 breasts with bone
3 medium onions
4 ribs celery
5 cloves garlic
2 bell peppers
1 small can tomato paste
1 large can tomatoes
½ lb. smoked Polish sausage
½ lb. sweet Italian sausage
½ lb. hot Italian sausage
Chili powder
Parsley flakes
Worcestershire sauce
Tabasco sauce
Salt and pepper
1 cup rice
3 bay leaves
Cayenne pepper

Boil chicken and sausage until tender—uncovered. Reserve and de-grease liquid. Saute chopped onions, celery, bell peppers, and garlic in light oil. Add cut-up chicken and sausage, tomatoes and tomato paste. Add seasoning to taste. (Don't scrimp on chili powder and cayenne pepper.) Cook for 30 to 45 minutes on low heat. Add 2 to 3 cups of reserved liquid and rice. Cook covered until rice is tender. (Rice eventually soaks up liquid nicely; but you can also cook rice separately as sometimes chicken and sausage get overdone from rice taking longer to cook than you might think.) Suggest using any and all hot sauces from River Run Restaurant, Plainfield, Vermont, 05667. Important: save some sausage for breakfast. Serves 8.

Howard Norman

LOUISE SHIVERS

Biographical statement, p. 24.

Louise's Backyard Gumbo

My grandson calls this my Backyard Gumbo because I like to make it when I can walk into the backyard and gather the tomatoes and okra for it where they are just at their peak. (No, no hothouse tomatoes or overlarge pulpy okra for me. If I can't find small tender okra, I don't make the gumbo.) I also like to make this when Vidalia onions are available.

This is what I consider a blissful day in the life of a writer: Piddle in the garden a little, cook a little, write a little . . . then gather the sweet ones around to eat and savor.

The actual recipe is one I found in the *South Carolina Writers' Project History* that was done in the 1930s. It was called "Okra Pilau" when I started playing around with it. Now I cook it in a heavy black cast iron frying pan I inherited.

Dice four slices of breakfast bacon and fry in deep pan until brown. Lift out bacon and place into the pan 1 chopped onion and 1 tablespoon chopped green pepper; then add 2 cups stewed tomatoes and 2 cups okra sliced thin (cut crosswise).

Let them cook down, stirring occasionally to prevent burning, and season with salt and pepper. Meanwhile, cook 2 cups rice in 2 quarts water with 1 teaspoon salt; after boiling 12 minutes, drain and mix with ingredients in the pan. Turn into serving boiler and steam for 20 minutes. Add bacon just before serving.

ROSELLEN BROWN

is the author of *Half a Heart, Before and After, Tender Mercies, The Autobiography of My Mother, Cory Fry, Cory Fry's Pillow Book, Some Deaths in the Delta,* and *Street Games.* She lives in Chicago.

Helen Bass Williams's Okra, Etc. Stew

This is a southern recipe, one that I learned from a wonderful woman named Helen Bass Williams, who taught alongside me and my husband at Tougaloo College in Mississippi in the mid '60s. It's not the kind of recipe that uses exact measures, so I'll be as informal as she was when she taught it to us; amounts can be approximate with no real loss. A lot of my northern friends hate okra but we're true southerners when it comes to the stuff, and this is one of the best recipes I've seen for it.

> Appox. 1 lb. okra, whole
> 1 large onion, sliced
> 1 or 2 green peppers, sliced
> Enough cabbage to cover the top of the above ingredients; more if you like it that way
> Butter or margarine, a generous dollop
> Salt to taste

Melt butter or margarine in the bottom of a heavy pot. Add okra, onion, peppers; cover with cabbage. Cook until everything's soft and stir. Salt to taste.

Rosellen Br—

TIM O'BRIEN

won the National Book Award in 1979 for his novel *Going after Cacciato*. He is the author of *The Things They Carried*, winner of the National Book Critics Circle Award, *In the Lake of the Woods*, and *July, July*.

Quick, Filling, and Pretty Good Chicken Soup

1. Cut up 2 carrots, 2 parsnips, and 2 celery stalks. Cook until medium-tender. Drain.
2. Open 2 cans of chicken noodle soup, preferably Progresso. Skim off fat. Dump soup into the pan of vegetables. Heat. Eat.

NIKKI GIOVANNI

is the author of more than fourteen books of poetry, including *Love Poems,* which won an NAACP Image Award. She is also the author of *My House* and *The Selected Poems of Nikki Giovanni.* She teaches at Virginia Tech.

The Most Wonderful Soup in the World

Soup, where I come from, is sacred . . . the food of the Gods . . . the most wonderful thing on Earth to eat because it is so hard to make. Canned soups and frozen soups and soups that you add water and stir—and I'm sure I don't even have to mention microwave soups— are not allowed in the house. My grandmother always told me the reason ghosts come back is somebody is either opening a can of soup or making a box cake. It was the very longest before I realized ghosts could come back for other reasons.

My mother, who is without doubt the world's best bean cooker, makes a mean soup, too. You need to know a couple of things about Mommy and me before I share this recipe. Mommy likes to save things. I'm sure it goes back to my grandmother. I don't. I'm sure it goes back to my father. My father was always single-mindedly focused. If he was polishing his shoes he'd just as soon take the tail of his good shirt to finish the shine. That drove Mommy crazy. I'm sort of like that. Mommy, on the other hand, will split a sheet of paper towel in half to get double the use and if she only used the half she used to do something like mop up a bit of water, she'd spread it on the countertop to dry and be used again. I moved back home because my father was diagnosed with colon cancer. So what we have is two women in one kitchen. Yo! A recipe for Frontier Soup or a recipe for disaster.

See, Mommy believes in saving grease. Grease. G R E A S E. Unbelievable. I don't do left-overs and especially not grease. I don't even cook with it. I would, therefore, throw the bacon grease out. She would hide it in the back of the fridge. I would find it and throw it out. She moved her can under the sink. We played that game for a couple of months. Me trying to convert her to olive oil; she trying to convert me to . . . grease. Now, Edna Lewis, whom I love, says you should cook with lard. Mommy pasted that article up all over the kitchen. But Miss Lewis, I tried to explain, means fresh lard. Fresh, smesh, lard is grease and grease is flavor. What is her book called? *In Search of Olive Oil*? I could fight Mommy. I could fight Grandmother. I could, if actually called to do so, fight Edna Lewis. I might even stand toe to toe with Scott Peacock. But not all of them at once. I was defeated. If I had to keep the grease, I would organize it.

I went downstairs and found a really beautiful large jar. I had, at one point, considered keeping pennies in it or goldfish, but now it was going to work for a higher cause: leftovers. If she was keeping grease then I would keep little snippets of whatever we ate. At first it was potatoes. I love boiled potatoes; they are, indeed, a gift from the gods. Then it was a bit of the roast, a bit of the chicken, a snippet of the pork chops. There were green things: green beans, greens, okra because I eat okra at least once a week, asparagus. My jar was filling up. There were squashes: zucchini, yellow squash, the squash with the neck. Eggplant, turnips, parsnips. We looked around at the end of the month and the jar was almost full. "Let's make soup," we said almost simultaneously. I ran to get a can of beer. There simply is no better starter. We emptied the leftover jar; we added one heaping tablespoon of grease (and by mutual agreement threw the rest away), a large onion, two large carrots, cut up green peppers, a head of garlic because there isn't any such thing as too much of a good thing. We added a large can of whole tomatoes, cut up some hot and sweet peppers, and went away. It cooked on low all afternoon. Periodically one of us would check to see if we should add water or beer . . . both work. At dinnertime we set a beautiful table . . . hot crusty bread with pesto for dipping. And the end-of-the-month-best-soup-in-the-world soup. I gotta tell you my son hated it. We made this dish once a month for all the time we lived together. My father liked it because it had so many flavors and textures. He thought it looked good but then he was sick. Gus, my father, would say, "Oh is the month over already?" And appear utterly delighted. Thomas would say, "Oh No! Not that soup again." Which just goes to show: there's no accounting for taste.

The key to this soup is courage. Mix and match your leftovers. That which cannot be made wonderful with beer will definitely yield to white wine. If all else fails: add milk and call it stew.

ANNE RIVERS SIDDONS

is the author of *Heartbreak Hotel, The House Next Door, Low Country, Up Island, Fault Lines, Nora Nora,* and *Peachtree Road.* She lives in Atlanta, Georgia.

Caldo Verde (Kale Soup)

I found this enclosed recipe on Martha's Vineyard, but it turns up wherever there are sizable Portuguese populations. Southerners in particular seem to love it; I think it's because it bears more than a passing resemblance to pot likker. In fact, it's wonderful with cornbread—a fact that has appalled more than one of my Downeast neighbors, until they try it.

      1 lb. fresh kale with stems, chopped
      ½ lb. chopped cabbage
      6 to 8 cups beef stock (or 3 cups beef broth and 3 cups canned vegetable broth)
      1 lb. *linguica* (Portuguese sausage) or any garlic flavored sausage; fat-free kielbasa
         will do fine
      ½ lb. *tasso* ham or country-cured ham
      2 garlic cloves
      1 cup chopped onions
      1 cup diced carrots
      3 cups diced new potatoes, unpeeled
      2 cups dark red kidney beans
      Salt and pepper to taste

Simmer the greens in the broth until tender. Add the sausage and ham and simmer an hour. Add the vegetables and simmer about 20 minutes more or until the potatoes are tender. Add the beans; season with salt and pepper. Add more broth, water, or wine if it needs more liquid.

Now for the fun part: Vineyarders toss in whatever leftovers they think would be good and refrigerate the soup until the next day. The best batch I ever made had a can of chicken broth with escarole tossed in, plus a cup or two of leftover lentil soup and a stiff slug of Merlot. White wine's good, too.

It freezes well and is a fine thing on a winter night.

Anne Siddons

JOHN T. EDGE

Biographical statement, p. 15.

Potlikker Consommé

Inspired by Huey Long

1 mess of collard greens, maybe mustards
1 smoked hog jowl or other smoked hunk of pig product
Salt to taste
Black pepper to taste
Homemade chicken stock, maybe a couple of pints
1 onion, chopped
Sherry and chopped, boiled egg (optional garnish)

Render some of the pork fat in a large stockpot. Remove the pork and set aside. Sautee the onion in the fat until the onion turns light golden. Add the chicken stock. Bring to a low boil. Add the pork and simmer for an hour.

Chop the greens and add to the pot. Simmer for 45 minutes to an hour. Strain the greens and pork.

Serve the consommé in teacups. Garnish with a bit of chopped egg, maybe a bit of ham pulled from the jowl, and, if you're feeling wild, the barest bit of sherry. Dunk cornbread.

KENNETH HOLDITCH

Biographical statement, p. 12.

Madame Begue's Collard Greens Soup

2 or 3 bunches young collard greens
1 cup small dry white beans
Fat salted pork
1 onion
3 cloves
4 garlic cloves
2 sprigs of thyme
Dash of hot pepper
2 cups diced Irish potatoes
2 quarts beef stock

Remove tender part of collards from stems. Wash and cut into shreds.

Parboil greens and beans separately.

Fry salt pork meat. Add onions, garlic, and a little flour and brown.

Pour in 2 quarts beef stock. Add collards, beans, and seasonings and bring to a boil. Simmer for 2 hours. Add diced potatoes in the last 20 minutes.

Serve with toasted bread.

Madame Begue opened a restaurant on Decatur Street in the French Quarter of New Orleans in the late nineteenth century and it became one of the best known eating establishments in the city. She is credited with having established the tradition of the Sunday brunch.

When I make this soup I sometimes use other greens, mustard or spinach, since it is difficult to get tender young collards and if they are not tender, they are rather like leather in the soup, no matter how long you cook them.

AMY BLOOM

is the author of *Come to Me,* a finalist for the National Book Award. Her work has appeared in the *New Yorker, Self, Vogue,* and *Talk,* among others. She lives in Connecticut and is a practicing psychotherapist.

Amy Bloom's Fool-Proof Matzo Ball Soup
Amaze Your Jewish Relatives; Please Your Baptist Friends

> 1 large fowl (the biggest your biggest pot can hold—don't forget it will be covered with water and surrounded by vegetables)
> A half-and-half blend of water and chicken broth, enough to cover said fowl
> Carrots, celery leaves, onions, chopped up and tossed into the pot
> Peppercorns and bay leaf (a few of each)

Put all into the pot and simmer for 3 or 4 hours, until the meat falls off the bone. Keep adding water to cover. Lift out carcass, chunks of meat, and vegetables. Stick in the fridge until the fat congeals. The next day, skim if off. Now you have really good chicken soup. At serving time, you can throw in a few cooked carrot rounds, a bit of the cooked chicken meat (whatever you didn't use for late-night snack, chicken salad, or chicken lasagna), or you can just leave it in its pure, golden glory.

Matzo Balls
> 1 package Manishevitz or Streit's Matzo Ball Mix

Follow the directions EXCEPT for several important deviations. After the Matzo meal-oil-egg goo has sat in the fridge for 15 minutes (not for 3 as the box says), before you start shaping the walnut-sized balls, add a tablespoon of plain club soda (seltzer, in my family). Admire the fizz and mix in, with your oil-coated hands.

Cook for 2 HOURS (not 20 minutes, as the box says). Give the blossoming matzo balls enough room to bobble around. Keep the lid on to keep their skins from drying out. Occasionally rotate them, with a delicate touch. Your house will smell great and people will keep you company in the kitchen, no matter how long you cook these things.

Cook them to death.

If you bring this soup and these matzo balls to the seder, you will be fussed over and admired. People will ask piercing questions about your lineage and men and women alike will cast yearning, wistful, inviting glances in your direction.

DARCEY STEINKE

is the author of the novel *Jesus Saves*. Her version of Song of Solomon will be published in the *Heretic's Bible*. She lives in Brooklyn with her daughter Abbie Jones and teaches at the New School for Social Research.

Leffert Garden Gazpacho

This cold soup is best in the summer months. You don't have to turn on the oven to make it but you do need a blender. As my daughter Abbie says, it's delicious and nutritious.

    Large can V-8 juice
    4 to 6 large vine-ripe tomatoes, peeled and chopped
    2 to 3 cucumbers, peeled and chopped
    2 large red onions, peeled and chopped
    6 cloves garlic
    1 red pepper, peeled and chopped
    1 ripe peach, peeled and chopped
    1 tablespoon chopped mint
    1 tablespoon sea salt
    1 teaspoon black pepper
    ½ cup olive oil
    3 tablespoons red wine vinegar

In a blender puree vegetables with V-8 juice. Pour into bowl and add all other ingredients and stir well. Chill for at least an hour and serve with a dollop of sour cream.

PATRICIA CORNWELL

spent six years working for the Virginia Chief Medical Examiner's Office and as a volunteer police officer before she wrote her first Dr. Kay Scarpetta novel, *Postmortem*. She is the author of nine subsequent Scarpetta novels, three police procedural novels, and most recently, *Portrait of a Killer*.

Miami-Style Chili with Beer

Anna, a friend of Kay's, invites Kay over to her house for dinner. Anna cooks up this chili with cans of chiles and garlic-spiked tomatoes that Kay brought from home from her last visit to Miami. This chili has the consistency of soup and is pleasantly spicy, since Kay uses the tame green (Anaheim) variety of chiles. However, you can crank up the heat by adding more chili powder and by passing a bottle of hot pepper sauce around the table.

Corona and Dos Equis are popular Mexican beers that will lend great flavor to this chili. If you have leftover chili, it freezes very well. Use airtight freezer containers, leaving ½ inch headspace at the top for expansion.

1 lb. lean ground turkey or extra-lean ground beef
3 tablespoons olive oil
1 ½ cups trimmed and sliced white mushrooms
1 ½ cups chopped green, red, or yellow bell peppers
1 cup chopped Vidalia or yellow onions
2 cloves garlic, minced
2 cans (28 ounces each) chopped tomatoes with diced green chilies
2 cans (16 ounces each) red kidney beans, rinsed and well drained
1 can (16 ounces) black beans, rinsed and well drained
1 bottle (12 ounces) Mexican beer
3 tablespoons red wine vinegar
2 tablespoons chopped fresh oregano or marjoram
2 tablespoons chopped fresh basil
2 bay leaves
1 ½ tablespoons chili powder
2 teaspoons salt
1 ½ teaspoons ground cumin
Coarsely shredded extra-sharp cheddar cheese for garnish

1. In large Dutch oven or 4-quart saucepan, cook the ground turkey in 1 tablespoon of the olive oil over medium-high heat for about 5 minutes, or until browned, breaking up the meat with the side of a spoon. Drain the turkey well. Transfer to a double layer of paper towels and press out the excess fat. Wipe out the pan.

2. In the same pan, heat the remaining 2 tablespoons olive oil over medium-high heat. Add the mushrooms, bell peppers, onions, and garlic and cook, stirring frequently, for 5 minutes, until the bell peppers are tender. Stir in the turkey, tomatoes with their juices, the kidney and black beans, beer, vinegar, oregano, basil, bay leaves, chili powder, salt, and cumin. Bring the mixture to a boil. Reduce the heat to medium and simmer, partially covered, for 1 ½ hours, stirring occasionally.

3. Taste the chili for seasoning. Remove the bay leaves. To serve, ladle the chili into bowls and top each serving with cheddar cheese.
Serves 8 to 10.

—Patricia Cornwell

TIM SANDLIN

has published six novels and written ten screenplays for hire. His most recent novel is *Honey Don't*. He lives in Jackson, Wyoming, with his family.

Potawatomie Chili

This recipe was told to me by a dying Potawatomie brave on an iceflow. Before he went over the falls, he said he had to pass on the ancient tribal chili recipe so that it would not die with him. Dances with Groundhogs' recipe calls for antelope burger, but I have found it works well with any ground game, regular lean hamburger, or even tofu burger.

    2 lbs. ground round
    Add microwave jackrabbit*
    3 onions, chopped semi-fine (or well)
    2 tablespoons chili powder
    1 tablespoon cumin

Simmer all this stuff until the burger is brown, then drain the excess fat.

Add:
    2 cans Wolf Brand chili (D W G was specific about the brand, but any canned chili
        without beans works. Potawatomies hate canned beans.)
    2 cans whole tomatoes (When adding the tomatoes, place each tomato in the palm of
        your hand and squeeze, allowing the pulp to flow between your fingers and into the
        chili. This gives a much more realistic consistency than cutting them up. Cutting
        them is the Seminole way.)

As the juice simmers, add another 2 tablespoons chili powder and 1 tablespoon cumin. Simmer to the thickness of alfalfa-fed buffalo do. Or as desired. Cheese and onions on top makes it even better.

* The original tribal recipe calls for jackrabbit but I tend to leave it out. Most of my guests don't want hare in their food.

STEWART O'NAN

was named one of Granta's Best of Young American Novelists. He is the author of *Everyday People, Wish You Were Here,* and *In the Walled City,* winner of the Drue Heinz Prize. He lives in Avon, Connecticut.

Flannery O'Connor Chili

1 whole boneless peacock (3 lbs.) or 3 lbs. boneless, skinned peacock breasts, cubed

2 medium onions

4 cloves garlic, chopped

½ cup peanut oil

½ cup chili powder

1 ½ teaspoons cayenne pepper

5 tablespoons ground cumin

¼ cup flour

3 large tomatoes

2 cups water

2 12-ounce bottles of Dixie beer

1 teaspoon cilantro

Juice of 1 lime

Go out in the yard at dark and listen in the trees. Catch one napping and bring it in. Knock it on the doorframe first, otherwise you're in for a time. Save the better feathers, you might use them later.

Cook the onions and garlic in the oil in a large pot, just to get some flavor out of them. Don't brown 'em! Toss in the cubes of meat and cook till they're white all around. Throw in your chili powder and cayenne and cumin and roll the meat around in it. Throw in your flour and roll it around again.

Puree the tomatoes and slop them in with one of the beers and then the water. Mix it up, turn the stove down, cover and simmer for 40 minutes. Stir in the cilantro and the lime juice. Take the lid off and simmer it another half hour.

Drink the other Dixie and taste the spoon so it burns your tongue good. Salt to taste, or more cayenne. Chili should be thick when it's ready.

Wear the feathers while you're eating. When you're done, go out in the yard with the pot and bang on it with a spoon. Holler "You're next, you lazy ingrates" so the neighbors can hear.

Yankees can substitute chicken. Real Yankees like Mr. John Cheever can substitute left-over Thanksgiving dinner.

GUY MARTIN

is a journalist currently in his twenty-ninth year of accidental exile from Alabama. He is at work on a book about the East German Secret Service during the Cold War. He lives in New York with his wife and daughter. (See page 10.)

Antelope Chili

This is a chili made from real chiles, the real way. No beans, all right? Don't waste time debating, just listen: It is a plate of red, made with the best meat for the job. Venison can substitute for antelope, but antelope is better. There are three classes of ingredients, those found in the high chaparral, those found in Mexico, and those found anywhere you are. The accomplishment of this chili is to meld them. Serves 10 to 12, or more, depending on how hungry people are.

Montana Ingredients
1) Go to Montana or some appropriate state in the upper West.
2) Wear some tough pants with double knees.
3) Crawl through the high prairie on your belly, cradling your gun.
4) Shoot the antelope.
5) When dressing the antelope, save the hams, backstraps, shoulders, and, if possible, a few ribs.
6) If you are in Montana, gather some wild sage.

Local Ingredients
1) Go to the store.
2) Buy 3 bunches of cilantro, many sprigs of fresh sage, 5 big Spanish onions, 2 medium-sized onions, 4 pounds beefsteak or plum tomatoes, 1 bunch of celery, 4 bell peppers, at least 2 heads of garlic, cumin, salt, peanut oil, olive oil.

Mexican Ingredients
1) Go to the Mexican food store (or go online).
2) Buy 12 oz. dried New Mexico chiles; 8 oz. dried ancho chiles; 2 to 3 cans chipotle chiles in adobo sauce; some Mexican oregano.

What to Do
A pronghorn is a big goat, basically. It's lean but has a thick fell over the muscles, so have your best knives out to deal with that. The fell must be entirely removed to make a tender

chili. The idea is to cook the three elements of the stew, partially, then let them marry as they cook the rest of the way together. It will take a day.

1) Get out your biggest pot. Chop the Spanish onions, celery, bell peppers, 4 or 5 cloves of garlic. Throw some butter, olive oil, and 3 or 4 pinches of Mexican oregano in the pot and cook the vegetables down slow.

2) Get out your biggest skillet. Sear 4 to 5 pounds of antelope (or venison), from the hams, shoulder, or backstraps, cubed in no more than 1-inch pieces, with olive oil, salt, and fresh sage. Be careful to leave the meat rare. Set aside, with pan juices.

3) If you have reserved the ribs of the antelope or the deer, chop 2 or 3 into a pot with a carrot, an onion, some sprigs of sage, and a clove of garlic, with 10 cups of water. Bring to a boil, then simmer for a couple of hours. The goal is to have 6 or 7 cups of fine antelope- or venison-flavored stock for use later. Chicken stock can substitute.

4) As the stock (in its pot) and the vegetables (in their pot) simmer, remove stems and seeds from all dried chilies, roast them for 5 minutes in a 250° oven. Heat a pot of 10 cups water (or less, if that will cover the chiles) almost to boiling, then turn off and immerse roasted chiles in the pot. A trick: find a plate or saucer of a diameter smaller than the pot and put it face-down in the pot on top of the chiles. They tend to float; this will force them to submerge. The water will blacken as the chilies rehydrate. This is the beginning of the chile sauce. Let stand.

5) Blacken the 4 pounds of tomatoes in a skillet. Separately, chop and saute the 2 medium-sized onions until brown.

6) Put blackened tomatoes, sauteed onion, rehydrated chilies, canned adobo chiles, (at least) 2 tablespoons adobo sauce, 2 ½ teaspoons cumin, 1 tablespoon Mexican oregano, 5 cloves garlic, and 1 tablespoon salt in a blender with 3 cups (or slightly more) of the reserved liquid from the rehydration of the dried chiles. CAVEAT: Taste chile water before using it. If it tastes sweet and hot, use it. If it tastes flat and bitter, use tap water instead. (There are few blenders this big, so mix the sauce and its spices in a pot and transfer to the blender in stages.) Puree to a fine degree, adding more chile water as desired, up to 4 cups. Reserve the remaining few cups of chile water. The sauce should now be the consistency of canned tomato sauce. Strain the sauce through a sieve, discarding all bits of chile skin that refuse to puree. This will take time. I like to work the sauce through the sieve with the back of a wooden spoon.

7) Refry the strained sauce for 4 minutes in a little peanut oil over high heat.

8) You're almost home. Add the chile sauce and the rare seared antelope (with its pan juices) to the big pot from step 1, above. Add 6 cups of the antelope or venison broth. If there's still not enough "room" in the chili for it to cook down, add a cup (or 2) of chicken stock.

9) Bring to a boil, then simmer covered, over low heat, for 2 hours, stirring frequently, adjusting salt, cumin, oregano, and sage as desired. As the chili thickens, gradually stir in (no more than) 2 more cups of the reserved chile water. Serve over white rice with chopped fresh cilantro atop the chili, flour tortillas, and cold lager beer.

DEE BROWN

(1908–2002) wrote more than twenty-five books on American history and the West. His works include *Bury My Heart at Wounded Knee*, *The American West*, and *Creek Mary's Blood*.

Permutable Chili

No specific chili recipe will ever be wholly accepted by any large group of diners. That is why when someone asks for my chili recipe, I give them this permutable formula, which allows a cook to experiment until a suitable mixture is developed.

Meat is the basic element of course. When vegetarians use eggplant or something else, the result is not chili. After all this is chili *con carne*. Beef is standard. Venison is excellent, having a pungent flavor of the wild. Some prefer goat, some mix in a bit of pork sausage. Some prefer their meat ground, others prefer it diced into small cubes. This recipe is for 4 people and calls for 2 pounds of whatever.

Start by chopping up 2 green peppers and 2 large onions . . . into a skillet containing 6 tablespoons of oil, stirring until brown, then add the meat, mixing in until all the red is gone. Those who like tomatoes should add about 3 cups, and, from this point on, be creative. Three teaspoons of garlic salt? Or regular salt and a clove of garlic? One-fourth teaspoon of paprika? One-fourth teaspoon crushed cayenne pepper? One-half teaspoon of Tabasco? Six whole cloves? Two large bay leaves?

Now we come to chili powder, of which there are at least a dozen commercial brands. Some gourmands prefer to mix their own. The basic ingredients are ground chili pepper, red pepper, oregano, cumin, and garlic. Usually one can find a prepared mixture suitable for one's taste buds. Four tablespoons are needed here.

The right flavors are essential, and additional ones, such as basil, can be added, in minute portions. A bit more oregano and cumin may add to the savoriness. H. Allen Smith once said that cumin was the most essential aroma in chili.

Some people like beans in their chili, others consider beans an abomination in chili. If beans are included, 2 cans of red kidney beans are called for in this recipe.

Now everything is ready to simmer, very slowly, for 2 hours, stirring only occasionally and perhaps adding a little water if needed.

When this chili was served to a visiting Oriental Indian, he expressed astonishment that the recipe for his favorite home dish had reached America. This stuff must be universal.

JIM LEHRER

won more than thirty awards for journalistic excellence for PBS's *The MacNeil/Lehrer Report* and anchors the news report renamed, after MacNeil's departure, *The NewsHour with Jim Lehrer*. He is the author of thirteen novels, two memoirs, and three plays.

North Texas Chili

I make North Texas Chili all the time. Besides, it's the only recipe I know how to make.

    2 lbs. lean ground meat
    2 good-sized cans stewed tomatoes
    1 green pepper, diced
    Chili powder to taste
    Salt to taste
    2 good-sized cans dark red kidney beans
    Grated Colby longhorn cheese
    Corn chips

In a large skillet or pot, brown meat. Drain grease. Add tomatoes, green pepper, onion, chili powder, and salt. Also, add a small amount of water.

Let the mixture simmer over a low heat for 1 ½ hours. Taste and adjust the seasonings, if, and when, necessary. Add the kidney beans and simmer for another 30 minutes.

Serve with grated Colby longhorn cheese and corn chips.

Serves 8 to 10.

ANNE RAPP

is a screenwriter who lives in Austin, Texas. She was a script supervisor for fifteen years before writing the movies *Cookie's Fortune* (which was nominated for an Independent Spirit Award and an Edgar Allan Poe Award) and *Dr. T and the Women.*

Hotter'n Hell Chili from the Lady of Falfurrias, Texas

I've been using the following recipe for twenty years. I adapt it occasionally to satisfy savory whims, but it's always just as good in its basic form. Its heat index is controlled by the amount of peppers that go in, but to me this chili will always be "hot" for one reason: I stole the recipe.

Twenty years ago I came across a cookbook from the Terlingua, Texas, Annual Chili Cook-off, considered by many the world championship of cook-offs. My favorite recipe was "Hotter'n Hell Chili." It won the cook-off in the early 1970s and was the creation of a lady from Falfurrias (pronounced *fal-furious*), Texas. For the life of me, I can't remember her name. I lost the cookbook during one of my numerous moves, so I can't look it up either.

I've often felt guilty that I shared this recipe with so many people under the guise of being mine. Especially since I can picture the Lady of Falfurrias furiously toiling at her big cast iron pot over a fire in the backyard in a 100° heat, days on end, perfecting it to the culinary state of world championship-ness so that I can now strut around in my air-conditioned kitchen, toss in a couple of extra gourmet purple garlic cloves or cluster tomatillos, call it my own, and be a hero.

Falfurrias is the county seat of Brooks County, located in far south Texas in the brush country of the Rio Grande plain. According to a nice lady from the Falfurrias Chamber of Commerce, the town got its name because an Indian once stood on a hill and spread his arms and yelled something that sounded like "Falfurrias!" and someone said, "What did he say?" and someone else said, "I don't know," but they decided to name the town that anyway. They later learned that "falfurrias"(to the Lipan brave's people) meant "the land of heart's delight." They were all very happy and the name stuck. (Heart's Delight is the name of a lavender wildflower that blankets the pastures of Brooks County every spring.)

Brooks County consists of 943 square miles and has a population of about 8,000. My old 1997 *Texas Almanac* lists their ethnic percentages as 82% White, 0.1% Black, 0.2% American Indian, 0.1% Asian, 17% Other, and 89% Hispanic. No famous mathematicians have ever come from Brooks County. The economy is based on oil, gas, cattle, hunting leases, grain sorghums, hay, and watermelons. The latest census shows the population of

Falfurrias at 5,297. (Being good at math, I used the above ratio to calculate that Falfurrias' 5,297 might include 4,344 whites and 4,714 Hispanics.)

Perhaps you're wondering what all this has to do with my chili recipe. I figure if I put all this stuff in about the town of its origin, maybe the Unknown Lady of Falfurrias won't be too furious at me for passing it off as mine in such a prestigious cookbook as this one.

Boneless chuck roast—cubed—brown on all sides—drain and put in chili pot.

Add tomato sauce (1 15-ounce can for every 3 pounds of beef).

Add a can of water for each can of tomato sauce.

Simmer about 15 minutes.

Add chili powder (about 5 tablespoons for 3 pounds of beef).

Add comino (cumin), oregano, garlic, salt, paprika (3 or 4 tablespoons cumin for 3 pounds of beef, the others to taste).

Sautee 1 or 2 medium white onions in Worcestershire sauce, then add to pot.

Add 1 or 2 ripe tomatoes, cut in chunks.

Add chopped jalapeno and serrano peppers, according to how hot you like it (remember the peppers get hotter the longer you cook them).

Optional: Add a small amount of chipotle peppers in adobo sauce. (It comes in a 7-ounce can and most markets have it.)

Bring this to a boil, then simmer covered. As it gets thicker, add beer. (Dos Equis is my choice.) Stir often to keep from sticking, adding beer when necessary.

After it has cooked for a few hours, add a bit of masa flour for thickness.

Begin the feast by standing on a chair and yelling "Falfurrias!"

One thing I do remember from the book: The Lady of Falfurrias supposedly waited until the judges were headed her direction and then she quickly doused the top of her chili with tequila and lit it, presenting it as *flaming* "Hotter'n Hell Chili," just like the famous desserts she'd heard about from Paris, France.

Anne Rapp

SEAFOOD

One of the best meals I ever had was cooked by Eugene Walter on a Bunsen burner in his Paris apartment, circa 1953. Max Steele was present. I can't recall what we ate, but I do remember Eugene crouching on the floor doing alchemical things around the flame. . . . I don't think he had a table.

— EVAN CONNELL

PAT CONROY

is the author of *The Water Is Wide, The Great Santini, The Lords of Discipline, The Prince of Tides, Beach Music,* and most recently *My Losing Season.* He lives in the low country of South Carolina with his wife, Casssandra King.

CASSANDRA KING

has published stories and essays in various quarterlies and anthologies. She is the author of *Making Waves in Zion* and *The Sunday Wife.* A native of L.A. (Lower Alabama) she now lives in the low country of South Carolina with her husband, Pat Conroy.

Dinner-Party Crab Casseroles

1 lb. white crab meat
2 boiled eggs, chopped
1 small onion, finely chopped
1 green pepper, chopped
Juice of 1 lemon
1 tablespoon Worcestershire sauce
2 raw eggs, beaten
½ cup Hellmann's mayonnaise
Fresh bread crumbs

Combine ingredients in mixing bowl, then spoon into individual mini-casseroles or shell-shaped backing dishes. Top with buttered bread crumbs. Bake for 30 minutes at 350° or until casseroles are set and bread crumbs golden brown.

PETE DEXTER

won the National Book Award for his novel *Paris Trout*. A columnist for the *Sacramento Bee*, he is also the author of *Deadwood* and *The Paperboy*.

This dish is entitled

The Wind Blew a Tree Down and It's Blocking the Driveway Again Cioppino

The first step, of course, and the most important, is the announcement: "Relax, Dian, I'll take care of dinner."

This can only be done when there's a tree across the driveway, by the way, so she can't escape.

We begin with two whole crabs. Claws, eyes, everything. They are prepared in this way: "Dian, would you mind just cleaning off those crabs, before you sit down?"

And while she's there, I mention it would be helpful if she'd scrub the clams (2 pounds) and peel the shrimp. There is 1 pound of shrimp, but I always buy big ones, so that separating them from their encasements isn't so time consuming.

At any rate, I clean everything—or have it cleaned—and then soak the clams a little while in salt water.

Then I cut up 2 or 3 onions, a carrot, and a little garlic and brown those things in oil.

After that, I cut a pound of swordfish or tuna or salmon into big pieces and drop that into the pot with the onions and carrots, etc. Right on top of that goes some tomatoes (beginning to feel the stress now, "All right, Dian, where are the damn tomatoes?") and I cook this for however long it takes to make the phone calls to get my friend Dr. Ploof to come to dinner (he is often involved with dental emergencies) and to bring his chain saw.

Once Dr. Ploof is on the way, I return to the pot and add chicken broth, some hot water, and those tough little green leaves you can't eat. I bring that all to a boil, adding a little salt, some black pepper, a couple of red chili peppers. This continues to boil for about a quarter of an hour, or until I hear the doctor firing up the chain saw. At this point, I add some clams and a little dry vermouth, and cook that another 5 minutes. Then the crabs and shrimp go in (you can almost hear the little fellows screaming) for about 15 minutes more, just as the doctor and his lovely wife walk in the front door, smelling of burnt wood. The smell, by the way, adds an outdoorsy ambience to dinner.

A salad tastes good with this, along with an ice-cold bottle of Boone's Farm apple wine.

GISH JEN

has contributed to the *New Yorker* and the *Atlantic Monthly.* Her work was chosen for *The Best American Short Stories of the Century.* She is the author of *Typical American, Mona in the Promised Land,* and *Who's Irish?* She lives in Massachusetts.

Mom's Shrimp Wonton

I've always wished I were a better cook than I am. I love to eat, and I particularly love to eat beautiful and delicious food with people I love. Unfortunately, though, I also love to talk, especially with people I love, and this generally leads to things going wrong. I have burnt so many pieces of innocent tasty salmon that I will have to come back as a large prized fish in my next life if there is any justice on earth. In this life I feel compelled to make sizable donations to fish hatcheries, and also to support marine sympathy in general. As a result of this, I have raised a son whose first stuffed animals were all whales.

Now I generally stick to simple foods that do not require more attention than they're going to get, for example: Mom's Shrimp Wonton. Shell and chop about 1 pound of shrimp. Add some sesame oil, some salt, some cornstarch, some sherry. You can also add some egg whites, or ginger, or ground pork, or chopped water chestnuts or scallions. Mix.

You will need a package of 50 wonton skins—available just about everywhere these days. Do not attempt to make the skins yourself unless you lack frustration in your life. Take each skin, place a scant teaspoon of the shrimp mixture smack in the middle, and fold in thirds. You will have a roll with a lump in its midsection. Flip your roll over and press the ends of the roll together, using a little water to make them stick. The result should look like a nurse's cap and will doubtless be familiar to you from a chop suey house of your childhood. Continue until you have used up all your shrimp mixture.

You can freeze the wonton at this point—on trays with a little flour—or, of course, you can prepare to eat them immediately. Throw them in boiling water and when the water boils again add ½ to 1 cup cold water. When the water boils again, the wonton are ready to be inhaled with a little chicken broth. Even my five-year-old will eat 10 of these in a sitting; I am generally too distracted to notice how many I am eating, which is just as well.

KAYE GIBBONS

is the author of *Ellen Foster, A Virtuous Woman, A Cure for Dreams,* and *Charms for the Easy Life.* She lives in Raleigh, North Carolina.

Shrimp and Grits Casserole

Grits for six—according to package directions
1 regular-size bar Cracker Barrel sharp cheese, grated
¾ cup milk
1 large egg
1 lb. medium shrimp, shelled and deveined
Seasoning salt
¾ stick butter, plus 1 tablespoon
¼ to ½ cup Italian bread crumbs

Preheat oven to 375°. Cook grits in a large saucepan. In a separate pan, saute shrimp in butter, sprinkle with seasoning salt (I use Jane's Crazy-Mixed-Up Salt). Melt grated cheese into the grits. Using a fork, mix egg into the milk and then pour mixture into the grits. Blend in the butter and stir until everything is blended. Fold in sauteed shrimp.

Pour onto a sprayed or buttered rectangular baking dish and sprinkle with the bread crumbs. Bake uncovered for 30 minutes or until golden and bubbly.

SHEILA BOSWORTH

is the author of two novels, *Slow Poison* and *Almost Innocent.* She is a graduate of Tulane University and lives in New Orleans.

Crevettes Désir (Shrimp Desire)

(Serves two, by candlelight)

Here in Louisiana, where it originated, this exquisite creation is sometimes known, unaccountably, as "Barbecued Shrimp." Yet it is not connected, in preparation or in taste, to any sane person's notion of "barbecue." It is a culinary masterpiece, the ingredients simple, the result sublime, and its powers extend far beyond the gastronomic. It is therefore called more fittingly "*Crevettes Désir.*"

Crevettes Désir not only fulfills the fervent demands of the most exacting aficionado of shellfish and sauces. It also sweetens harsh voices, softens stubborn wills, and resurrects moribund honeymoons. One taste changes troublesome husbands into docile lapdogs, compels aging bachelors to marry, and renders wild young women wise. Its rich aroma dazzles haughty in-laws and drives to despair clinging mistresses and vindictive wives desperate for the recipe. *Crevettes Désir* should be prepared only by those who truly desire an irrevocable effect, as did a certain great beauty in New Orleans who, bored with being treated as a plaything, fed the dish one Twelfth Night to her married lover. Instantly upon tasting it, his heart began to beat in a new rhythm, one that was perfectly attuned to every desire of the lady's heart. But she, having brought him to his knees, let him go. Many years later, a very old man, he came again to her door on another winter's night to beg a second chance. And again she sent him away, refusing to speak to him of their final dinner together, denying him a last taste of the sea shrimp, redolent with rosemary, that had wrecked his life. He went off into the darkness, twice ruined.

NB: Do not allow yourself to be tempted to alter or augment the ingredients, or to vary the method of cooking. And never feed *Crevettes Désir* to anyone in whose dreams, for good or ill, you are unwilling to remain forever.

Preheat oven to 325°.

2 lbs. of large shrimp, taken fresh from the Gulf of Mexico
1 lb. (4 sticks) of good margarine (butter will burn)
Fresh black pepper (not coarse-ground)
Rosemary leaves (to be found at any grocery store, in the spices section, not the produce department)
Fresh bay leaves

Do not peel the shrimp or remove the heads. Place the shrimp in a colander and rinse with cold water; drain. Place a layer of shrimp in a wide, shallow pan (for instance, an ordinary broiler pan with the chrome broiling rack removed). Sprinkle the shrimp with a great amount of black pepper. Lace the shrimp liberally with rosemary. Place several bay leaves atop the shrimp. Slice one entire stick of margarine into squares and scatter the squares atop the shrimp. Repeat this process exactly with the next layer of shrimp, until the pan is filled. DO NOT ADD SALT UNTIL AFTER THE SHRIMP HAVE FINISHED BAKING AND HAVE BEEN REMOVED FROM THE BAKING PAN. The salt will lock the shrimp into their shells and make peeling them difficult.

Place the pan of prepared shrimp into the preheated oven and set the oven timer for 13 minutes. At the end of 13 minutes, with a large cooking spoon turn the shrimp to allow their other sides to become pink. Reset the timer for an additional 13 minutes. When a total of 26 minutes has passed, remove one of the largest shrimp from the pan and taste it. It should spring easily out of its shell and be firm without being hard. If the shrimp is hard, cook for an additional 3 minutes, then test again.

With a slotted spoon, removed the baked shrimp to a large serving platter. Pour the extravagant juices that have formed in the pan into individual serving bowls. Add to the sauce salt to taste.

The shrimp are to be peeled and eaten by hand, and the sauce which drips onto the fingers may be licked off. Do not hesitate to suck the heads.

Serve *Crevettes Désir* with warm, crisp French bread for dipping into the sauce, along with a salad of endive studded with ripe olives and dressed with a good Dijon vinaigrette. A fine, chilled Chardonnay and a dessert of fresh fruit and warm Brie are fitting accompaniment and finale.

ANDREI CODRESCU

is a National Public Radio commentator on *All Things Considered*. He edited *Exquisite Corpse: A Journal of Books and Ideas* and is the author of *The Blood Countess, A Muse Is Always Half-Dressed in New Orleans, No Tacos for Saddam,* and *The Devil Never Sleeps.*

Transylvanian Shrimp Creole

(try this at home at your own risk)

   2 Bloody Marys
   2 lbs. of medium shrimp
   4 Creole tomatoes
   2 large green peppers
   1 sweet red pepper
   5 bay leaves
   8 cloves of garlic
   5 teaspoons Hungarian paprika
   Tony Chachere's Creole Seasoning
   Cornmeal for polenta

Drink a Bloody Mary for mood. Boil shrimp for 2 minutes in water with bay leaves, salt, pepper, garlic, celery, and Tony's. Keep stock. Peel shrimp, set aside. Saute garlic and green and red pepper briefly—keep crunchy. Add tomatoes, bay leaves, and stock and simmer for 10 minutes. Add shrimp. Simmer 1 minute, remove from fire. Start on your second Bloody Mary and prepare polenta. Sprinkle cornmeal in boiling water constantly with a wooden spoon until thick, salting with the sweat on your forehead. Let it sit until it gets even thicker. Stir the Hungarian paprika in the mush and bake for 10 minutes. Cut polenta cakes for each plate and pour the shrimp creole on top. Say your prayers backwards and eat.

   Hope you try it, it's good.

DAVID GUTERSON

won the PEN/Faulkner Award for his novel *Snow Falling on Cedars*. His books include *The Country Ahead of Us, The Country Behind,* and *East of the Mountain.*

Geoduck Strips

The proper pronunciation is "gooeyduck," an enormous clam native to the North American west coast from Alaska to Baja, California, but most abundant in British Columbia and in my home waters of Puget Sound.

The geoduck is phallic in appearance, undeniably so. Its neck, or siphon, is often as long as three feet. Certain people find it disgusting; these are the same people who won't eat chicken liver mousse, squid salad, steamed mussels, or Louisiana Crayfish Boil.

Geoduck meat divides neatly into two categories. The neck, a muscle, is a fatless protein, chewy in texture unless properly prepared, subtle to the taste but ultimately superior to the rich and fat-laden breast meat, which is always tender and loud.

Geoduck is currently quite fashionable as sushi, its neck meat sliced into delicate slivers and served with rice and wasabi. Prepared in this manner, it tastes vaguely sweet, something like a cantaloupe but with the coarse, chewy texture of a carrot. Another approach, less faddish and less interesting, is geoduck breast served as an abalone-like steak, often sautéed in margarine. Indigenous grassroots Northwest preparations include geoduck fritters, geoduck chowder, and geoduck flamed in sake.

Geoduck Strips demand a fortuitous conjunction of circumstances and a heightened feeling for the miserable truth behind this stalwart adage: you only go around once in life.

The recipe starts with a neighbor pointing out at mid-morning of a summer's day that a minus tide is imminent. A general consensus gathers itself—let's go get some geoducks. Shovels and children are soon found. A digging party is haphazardly assembled—someone's nephew, a self-appointed expert, a perennial novice, a sullen teenager. Someone enthusiastic goes to town for limes. Someone else peeks into the freezer to ensure that enough ice is handy.

An hour passes. The diggers bring their catch from the beach. The clams are laid in the kitchen sink with their necks drooping phallically over the side. A neighbor's aunt, astonishing everyone, begins to make obscene jokes.

The clams are doused in boiling water. More neighbors appear. Someone gets serious about making gin and tonics. The radio gets turned on.

The breast is carved away from the stomach. The neck is laid open from end to end and slapped on the chopping block. Someone runs across the road for one of those meat tenderizing hammers with the pulverizing faces. Then a woman, generally, is called upon to beat the neck meat mercilessly while the men watch on in abhorrence. The muscles are destroyed, the meat made soft. Now the day is about geoduck clams. It is late afternoon and nothing necessary has been accomplished. No one really cares.

The Basic Directions
Cut the neck meat into pieces the size of Bazooka-brand bubble gum and lay on a plate. Cut the breast meat into similar-size pieces and lay them out on a second plate.

Dip the meat in beaten egg and dust with bread crumbs, salt, and pepper. Start two skillets on medium high heat. Pour olive oil, a sensible amount, in each. Saute meat in separate pans, turning once, prodding now and then with a long fork for no particular reason other than a nervous cooking style. Neither over- or under-cook. This is not difficult to do.

Arrange meat on warm serving platters, keeping breast and neck meat separate. Garnish with attractive lime wedges. Freshen everybody's gin and tonic. Turn up the radio. Give everyone a toothpick. Put the geoduck platters on porch table. Eat with sandy feet.

ANN PATCHETT

won the 2001 PEN/Faulkner Award for her novel *Bel Canto*. She is also the author of *The Patron Saint of Liars, Taft,* and *The Magician's Assistant.* She lives in Nashville, Tennessee.

Salmon on Spinach

This is very easy, very fast, and very good. I've made it for 8 people at a dinner party, and while assembly-line experience is helpful putting together so many pieces, it does work for large groups. This version serves two.

Sesame-Ginger Vinaigrette
(This is from my plastic Williams Sonoma dressing cruet with fine dressing recipes printed on the side. I highly recommend it.)

  3 tablespoons rice wine vinegar
  2 tablespoons soy sauce
  2 tablespoons honey
  ½ teaspoon dark sesame oil
  1 teaspoon sesame seeds
  2 teaspoons grated fresh ginger
  4 tablespoons canola oil

  2 pieces of salmon, approximately ⅓ lb. each
  1 large yellow onion
  1 teaspoon olive oil
  ½ lb. or more fresh baby spinach leaves
  1 small log of goat cheese
  1 pink grapefruit

Slice the onion as thinly as possible and caramelize it by cooking in a heavy pan over low heat with a teaspoon of olive oil, stirring frequently. When the onion is quite brown and completely limp, set it aside. It can take 45 minutes. You can cook it right up until the dish is ready to be assembled or briefly re-heat it at the last minute.

Preheat oven to 425°. Seed and section the grapefruit and put the sections aside. Place the washed and dried salmon in a shallow pan and top with whatever juice you can squeeze out of the grapefruit rinds. Let it sit for ten minutes. In the meantime, make the vinaigrette. Crumble the goat cheese into a small bowl and set aside.

Bake the salmon in the hot oven for 10 to 18 minutes, depending on how cooked you like your fish. While the fish is cooking, lightly steam the spinach. Be careful, as over-steamed spinach can reduce to about a tablespoon. This should just be wilted. Gently squeeze spinach and put it on 2 warm plates, top with salmon fillets (be sure to remove the skin when you take it out of the pan), top the fish with the caramelized onions, top the onions with goat cheese, top the goat cheese with grapefruit sections, then drizzle some well-shaken vinaigrette onto the whole thing. Serve immediately. This dish counts as a salad, a meat, and a vegetable, so don't worry about supplying anything but bread, wine, and possibly a light dessert.

Ann Patchett

JIMMY BUFFETT

is an author, singer, and songwriter. His books include *Tales from Margaritaville, Where Is Joe Merchant?* and *A Pirate Looks at Fifty.* He has recorded more than thirty albums. His songs include the hit singles "Margaritaville" and "Come Monday."

Fast Boat to China

I first came across the Shanddong style of preparing fish at Legal Seafood in Boston. It is a spicy, tangy accent that can be used with just about any kind of fish. It works just as well on a filet of striped bass in Long Island as it does on a piece of fresh grouper in the Bahamas, and even catfish for you landlocked chefs. It is fast and easy to do, but with all fish, remember not to cook it the way you remember it prepared in high school cafeterias. Great fish requires a minimum of time on the heat. It is not that far from bait to plate when it comes to cooking fish.

The Fish
Catch or buy a fish. Catching is a lot more fun and a lot more expensive. If you get addicted to the catching part like I am you can figure out that you will probably be paying close to $500 an ounce of meat after you include the price of your boat, tackle, outfits, fuel, and a million other totally necessary things you need to be an accomplished fisherman.

Cleaning the Fish
Scaling and cleaning fish is not something that most people really like to do. All it does is add to the total involvement in the process from ocean to plate if you are someone who enjoys that kind of thing. Whether you clean and filet your fish or just go to the local fish market and buy it, you want your filets to be ½ to ⅓ inch thick.

The Sauce
  2 cloves of crushed garlic
    I prefer to pan roast the garlic a little to begin with. It sweetens the garlic and allows people to stand closer than fifteen feet away from you after dinner, but if you want a lingering memory of your dinner, raw garlic is fine.
  2 tablespoons of chopped fresh ginger
  1 large handful of chopped cilantro
  ⅔ cup of soy sauce

Dash of hot sauce

I prefer a very spicy sauce from Trinidad called Matouks. It comes in a ketchup bottle but don't be fooled. DO NOT POUR IT LIKE KETCHUP. Any good gourmet shop should have it, but if you can't find it we carry it at the Margaritaville Store in Key West (1-800-COCOTEL). For the faint of heart or those lost in the wide open spaces far away from such things, Krystal or Tabasco will do.

Juice of 1 whole fresh lime

Mix this all together and pour half the marinade over the fish and let stand in the fridge for 30 to 60 minutes.

Grill on an open fire, usually 6 to 7 minutes, basting the filets two or three times.

Extra sauce can be thickened by adding a bit of cornstarch until you get the consistency of a good brown gravy. Remove the fish from the grill, pour the sauce over the fish, and garnish with fresh chopped shallots and a dash of finely grated lime peel.

Serve with yellow or coconut rice. Steamed broccoli or asparagus goes well with this dish.

HOWARD FRANK MOSHER

is a Vermonter and the author of seven novels.

Northern New England Brook Trout

A warm day in late May
A mess of brook trout
½ cup of flour or cornmeal (optional)
A little butter
A frying pan

Go to a small brook in May when the black cherry trees are in blossom. Catch half a dozen brook trout. Use worms for bait. Flies are for sissies and flatlanders. Put a few wild mint leaves in your creel with the trout to keep them fresh. Build a small fire beside the brook. If you live where a permit is required to do this, move further north. Clean the fish. Dip your trout in the flour or cornmeal if you feel like it. Fry them in real butter for 4 or 5 minutes on a side, or until the tails curl up crisp. Eat them with your fingers, with bread and butter and strong black coffee.

I first began eating freshly caught brook trout cooked beside the stream when I was a very small boy. Fishing tiny meadow and mountain brooks and eating the trout right out of the water still makes me feel like a kid again. It connects me to my family, especially my father and uncle, who taught me how to catch and fry up brook trout, and to the beautiful countryside where brook trout live. And as my logging and woodsman mentor Jake Blodgett used to say, "Pan-sized trout are the best eating fish in the world."

—Howard Frank Mosher

HOWELL RAINES

is the former executive editor of the *New York Times.* He won the 1992 Pulitizer Prize for feature writing. His works include *Whiskey Man,* a novel, *My Soul Is Rested,* and *Fly Fishing through the Midlife Crisis.*

Smoked Trout a la Redge Hanes

Go to Iceland.

Find the better of the two fly shops in Rekyavik.

Buy a stainless steel smoker like the one Redge Hanes got there several years ago and keeps at Cane River in North Carolina. It's about 18 inches long and 12 inches wide and 8 inches high. Mine did not come with instructions, so you can follow these if you have the same luck.

Set up the contraption in the yard and fill the pan in the bottom of the smoker with the wood chips they sold you in Rekyavik.

Catch a rainbow trout, gut it, leaving the fish whole and the head attached. Scale. Salt the fish inside and out.

Put it on the rack inside the smoker and clamp the lid in place. Open the little vent on top that allows smoke to escape. Fill the burners under the wood pan with denatured alcohol and light them. Let them burn until the fuel is gone.

Admire the fish and then peel off its brown skin. Serve hot or cold.

Makes a nice fish salad with capers, onions, and mayonnaise, too.

Howell Raines

BOBBY CLEVELAND

has been a sports writer for twenty-eight years and has served for the past sixteen years as outdoors editor of the *Jackson Clarion-Ledger.* He is well known as a chef of wild game and fish and has contributed recipes to many cookbooks.

Really Red Snapper

This recipe works wonderfully with red snapper, but is good with any firm saltwater fish or larger freshwater fish like largemouth bass, hybrid striped bass, or catfish.

> 2 or 3 lbs. of snapper filets, about ½ or ¾ inches thick
> Cavender's green seasoning
> 1 cup flour
> 3 fresh tomatoes, sliced thin
> 1 cup freshly grated Parmesan cheese (do not substitute canned cheese)
> 1 cup sliced almonds
> ¼ cup chopped green onion tops
> ¼ cup chopped fresh basil leaves
> Olive oil
> Pam or other non-stick spray

Thirty minutes prior to cooking, take filets out of refrigerator and season each filet thoroughly with Cavender's, massaging it in with fingertips. Allow fish to sit until it comes to room temperature, about 30 minutes.

Preheat oven (with a broiler) to 450°.

Turn eye on stove to medium high.

Spray a large non-stick frying pan with Pam, then pour enough olive oil to thinly coat the bottom of the pan and place on medium high heat.

Season the flour with Cavender's, whisking it to mix thoroughly, and then dredge each filet to lightly cover both sides of the fish. Saute the filets on both sides until crispy, but not until done, about 2 minutes per side. Repeat process until all filets are done, but it is best to cook all the fish at the same time (even if it requires two pans).

Spray Pam in a Pyrex baking dish (use one large enough to hold all the fish snuggly) and place the fish on bottom. Cut the pieces if necessary to give an even fit.

Cover the fish with a layer of sliced tomato, making sure not to overlap the tomato slices.

Scatter the chopped basil over the tomatoes, then cover the dish with the almonds. Top the almonds with the grated cheese and the green onion.

Place on an upper rack in a 450° oven for 1 minute to finish cooking the fish and to roast the almonds and tomatoes. Turn the oven to broil and vent the door. Broil until almonds and cheese turn golden, but not brown. Do not overcook.

Serve, like a casserole, with a spatula.

Variations: Try adding a layer of slightly wilted spinach leaves (cooked in white wine) on the bottom of the baking dish. Grilled thin slices of eggplant or zucchini can be used instead of or in addition to the tomato. Freshly grated Asiago cheese can be substituted for Parmesan cheese, but never substitute canned cheese for freshly grated hard cheese.

CHRISTOPHER BUCKLEY

is a novelist and editor of *Forbes FYI* magazine. His books include *Thank You for Smoking*, *Wry Martinis*, and *Little Green Men*. He lives in Washington, D.C.

Heart-Stopping Shad Roe

1. Buy shad roe.
2. Wash shad roe.
3. Dredge (cooking word for drag) shad roe through flour seasoned with black pepper and a dash of cayenne—not too much.
4. Cook bacon in iron skillet until nice and crisp. (Important: Don't throw out grease.)
5. Put shad roe in hot grease. Cook until browned on both sides or until individual shad roe eggs start to explode like miniature grenades. Cover face.
6. Remove shad roe from skillet.
7. Squeeze lemon copiously over shad roe. Crumble bacon on top. Serve with buttered new potatoes and dill and salad and crisp sancerre wine.
8. Enjoy.

RUDOLFO ANAYA

is a professor emeritus of English and creative writing at the University of New Mexico. He is the author of *Bless Me, Ultima*, *Heart of Axtlan*, *Zia Summer*, and *Jalamanata*.

Sardinas de Lata (Sardines from the Can)

I don't know where to begin my praise of a mouth-watering sardine sandwich after a long morning of writing, especially if the novel is going nowhere. It begins with the opening of the can. There is an art to opening the can without spilling the precious oil in which the tasty friends are packed. I suggest each person experiment with the process, and do share it with a loved one. That first essence of sardines can be intoxicating.

A pre-sandwich aperitif is a shot of tequila.

Gingerly removed each sardine from its oily home and place them lengthwise on a warm tortilla. Add hot mustard, your preference, and thick slices of onions. I prefer Vidalia onions to complement the green chile which has been prepared with plenty of garlic.

A person can write all day on an easy to fix sardine sandwich. If you can't find green chile at your deli, add extra Dijon mustard.

As to the brand, I buy American; Portuguese sardines are for connoisseurs. I do love slightly smoked sardines, but today sardines come in a variety of sauces, so I leave that exploration of fine dining up to each sardine lover. Go on, don't be afraid to explore; I trust you'll find the right sardine flavor you can share with your friends.

The complimentary drink is a stout beer. Californians prefer a Chardonnay, full bodied, gay and busy, and with a nutty flavor. Don't sweat the bouquet because the sardines will kill it. Quite honestly, if a royalty check has just arrived and there's a hardy Merlot or Cabernet in the house, these reds pull their weight with sardines.

Palette cleanser: I take another shot of tequila. If you're on your way to meet your agent or publisher (which few of us are nowdays) breath mints will do. A caution, breath mints do tend to clash with the satisfying aftertaste of sardines.

(If you thought I was going to give a recipe for tacos or enchilades, plates laden with spicy New Mexico chile verde or chile colorado as only my wife can prepare, sorry. When left alone to my devices and deep in a novel I go for the quick and easy to prepare protein. Su amigo de Nuevo Mexico, where we have never heard the phrase, "We sail with the tide." Ciao.)

BEVERLY LOWRY

is the author of six books, including *Come Back, Lolly Ray, Crossed Over,* and *Her Dream of Dreams.* She is a professor at George Mason University.

Anchovy Anything

I love food, especially in dreamiest times of wild imagining. I think about food all the time; like food just-about anything: food movies, food conversations, cookbooks, food you name it. I especially love to plan dinner parties—the guest list, the menu, what to put on the table for dessert which will involve no work at all—and like to shop and chop (love how the smells emerge and rise) and make the table nice. I even get pleasure from strategizing the cooking (speaking out loud to myself as I go) so that all the dishes get to the table at the same time. Eating's a kind of comedown, after all the anticipation and lush fantasizing. But eating's good, certainly.

If I had to choose one taste to have the rest of my life—a kind of food eternity—I'm pretty sure I'd choose roasted peppers with olive oil, anchovies, and fresh basil. The only problem with serving this dish at a dinner party is I never get enough, and there aren't any leftovers. Here's how I do it.

Roast whole bell peppers all over, under the broiler. (I like a combination of colors, red, green, and yellow, but mostly red, which to my mind are fleshier and have the most taste.) Turn them, watch them. Let the skin get wrinkled and a little burned. Takes 10 or 15 min-utes. Pop them into a brown paper sack, to cool. When you take them out, the skin of the peppers will have lost its starch, and you can peel it off pretty easily. Toss the skin. Slice the peppers thickly, but do *not* wash them, as some recipes instruct. If small flecks of black skin insist on sticking around for the main event, indulge their wish and give them a break. (I kind of like a little taste of burnt, myself.) Arrange the pepper slices on a pretty platter (black is nice) in a pattern that is color confident and which completely pleases your eye. (Sequence is important. If you don't do this in the order given, you're on your own, but don't come whining to me with complaints. Not that I'm cranky. But one true fact which no sane mind would deny is recipe-makers and head cooks get to be tyrants. Bossiness being their deepest nature.)

Scatter bits of anchovies across the top of the gorgeously arrayed peppers. (I like to tear the little things apart instead of cutting them.) Salt them with kosher salt but not too much, because the anchovies are salty. (Especially Reese's, which to my mind are too salty.) Pepper them with fresh-ground pepper. Pour very good extra-virgin olive oil on top, then place many gently torn and unbruised leaves of fresh basil across the top of the dish. Lots of basil. Be liberal with everything. In cooking, as in all worthwhile pursuits, fearlessness is of the essence and instinct is everything.

Stand back and look. Food is not just food. Its pleasures are various, and like Cleopatra, they never grow pale, or become old hat. Diddle with the arrangement of basil until you are completely satisfied. Serve with grilled chicken, leg of lamb, pork tenderloin. Serve as a first course, if you do that kind of thing. (I prefer everything at once, eaten exactly in the order I choose.) Serve in place of meat for vegetarian friends. Eat on crusty bread as a sandwich. Eat and eat.

As for anchovies, I can't get enough. I make anchovy everything except ice cream. Used to be, before serving anchovies, I'd ask guests in advance if they liked them. It's a crucial question, about which people are never ambivalent. I once fed sliced, home-grown tomatoes with anchovies to Larry McMurtry. The fastest motion since Ali's hook was that writer getting the salty fish out of his mouth. But he didn't complain. And we're still friends. Time to time, I have considered staging an anchovy test for new acquaintances, to see whether or not we can be friends because if they don't like anchovies, why bother? But that seems a little harsh. And remembering McMurtry, I don't. But it's a thought I still sometimes have.

POULTRY & GAME

My cat, Sneaky Pie, is writing a cookbook for cats,
but I don't think dried mole would be appetizing.

— RITA MAE BROWN

MARK BOWDEN

is the author of *Black Hawk Down,* a finalist for the 1999 National Book Award. His other books include *Killing Pablo, Bringing the Heat,* and *Doctor Dealer.* He lives in Pennsylvania.

This recipe was submitted by Mark's wife, Gail Bowden, who recalls, "True story: he nearly burnt down his house while making it for me when we first started dating, a looooong time ago!"

Mark Bowden's Kung Pao Chicken

4 boneless, skinless chicken breast halves

For the Marinade:
   1 egg white, beaten lightly
   2 teaspoons cornstarch
   2 tablespoons soy sauce
   1 tablespoon rice wine
   ½ teaspoon salt

For the Stir-fry Sauce:
   2 teaspoons cornstarch
   2 teaspoons rice wine
   2 tablespoons soy sauce
   1 tablespoon vinegar
   ½ teaspoon salt
   2 teaspoons sugar

For the Stir-fry:
   2 to 3 tablespoons sesame oil
   2 to 6 dried red chili peppers, depending on taste
   2 tablespoons grated fresh ginger root
   2 to 3 green onions, sliced
   ¼ cup peanuts

Cut the chicken breasts into 1- to 2-inch pieces. Place chicken in a plastic or glass bowl. Mix together all marinade ingredients and pour over chicken pieces. Stir and let marinate for about ½ hour.

Prepare ingredients for stir-fry, then pour sesame oil into wok or large frying pan. Heat over medium high heat and add red peppers according to desired spice level: 2 for mild, 4 for medium, and 6 for a hot dish! When peppers start to blacken, remove from oil and discard. Remove chicken pieces from marinade and add to oil. Stir-fry for a few minutes, then add remaining stir-fry ingredients and cook until chicken is done. Add stir-fry sauce and heat until sauce is bubbling.

Serve with rice. Makes 4 servings.

PATTY FRIEDMANN

Biographical statement, p. 20.

Recipe for Entire Chicken

My daughter was conceived on an entire chicken, though a pitcher of margaritas didn't hurt. I call the recipe "Entire Chicken" because of that exquisite lament in "A Thousand Clowns": "I can't do anything right. Last night I burned an entire chicken."

This even I can do right.

1 whole frying chicken
Pam

Cover shallow baking pan with foil and place small rack in the center. Spray rack with Pam. Empty chicken cavity of all jetsam someone in Mississippi or Arkansas thought would be fun to send you. Plop chicken on rack. Spray with Pam. (If you're a show-off, feel free with salt and pepper.) Place in preheated 350° oven for 1 ½ to 2 hours. It's done when leg wiggles—with help.

Best if eaten straight from oven without utensils. Or napkins.

Serves two . . .

NICHOLAS DAWIDOFF

is the author of *The Catcher Was a Spy, The Mysterious Life of Moe Berg, In the Country of Country,* and *The Fly Swatter.* He lives in New York City.

Rebecca's End of a Long Day Roast Chicken (And How to Get Her to Make It)

> 1 wife whose tiring job makes her disinclined to cook your favorite dish (her sensational roast chicken)
> 1 husband with a jones for said roast chicken
> 1 chicken

Time: 2 quality hours

1. Look wan, pallid, and malnourished and be unable to imagine why you feel so enervated.
2. Beg for "glorious," "delicious," "all-restoring" roast chicken. (Some cooks like to sprinkle in references to "my Mom" who "sweetly offered" to "send a chicken over," but this is a delicate procedure not recommended for novice chefs.)
3. Rush off and buy the provisions. (State that mere thought of her chicken provided energy to do so.)
4. Agree to clean up and wash dishes. (Brillo pads helpful for grotty roasting pans.)
5. Agree to provide 1 massage. (2 handfuls of shoulder, knead thoroughly.)
6. Agree to no in-house mention of the word baseball for full week next season. (Preferable to do this before September/October when the games are most important, unless you are a Tampa Bay Devil Rays fan in which case it is best to avoid April, the only month when games are meaningful.)
7. Agree to be neat in the bathroom. (If this strikes you as too ambitious, offer to install one of those new Japanese toilets with the self-closing seat and automatic bird twitter.)
8. Agree to clean Mitzy's litter box.
9. Agree to send Scofflaw (your dog) for a free range vacation with out of state friends.
10. Promise to resume jogging.
11. Claim always wanted to go with her to that dress shop she's been mentioning. (To avoid accusations of disingenuousness, toss in a pinch of expertise such as, "You know, the place that hems against the bias.")

12. Offer to forgo television for whole weekend and instead rent entire Merchant/Ivory video oeuvre. (Here best to claim ignorance of "this" Helena Bottom (cq) Carter.)

13. Agree to re-zoning of bed surface geography.

14. Agree to cease "slamming things around" every time President's name mentioned in event he is a Bush.

15. Agree to forever be unbothered by mentions of her old swain Willie Wunderkind (baste with ⅔ cup of restraint whenever phrase "just friends" causes simmering).

16. Agree to consider merits of soy products.

17. Offer to put other "chicken" in other "oven" and "bake" (ya know what I'm sayin').

18. Confess that she was right after all.

19. If all has failed, set oven on 400°, insert chicken and roast. Yield: 4 servings. Season to taste.

BAILEY WHITE

is a commentator on National Public Radio's *All Things Considered.* Her works include *Quite a Year for Plums, Mama Makes Up Her Mind: And Other Dangers of Southern Living,* and *Sleeping at the Starlight Motel.* She lives in South Georgia.

This Is a Chicken Recipe

Step 1

> 3 cups chicken stock
> 1 tablespoon sugar
> 1 teaspoon ginger
> ½ cup soy sauce
> ½ cup sherry
> 1 onion, chopped up
> 1 4 to 5 lb. chicken

Combine all ingredients except chicken and bring to a boil. Add chicken, cover and boil for 15 minutes. Remove from heat and let sit covered for 20 minutes.

Step 2

> ½ cup grated coconut (not the sweetened kind)
> A nub of ginger, chopped up small
> 1 teaspoon thyme
> A chunk of tamarind

Degrease the liquid from step 1. (Take the chicken out and set it aside for this step). Boil the tamarind and when it is soft enough mesh it through a sieve. Mix up the coconut, ginger, thyme, and tamarind into the liquid from step 1 and boil it down until it's rich and thick. In the meantime cut up the chicken and brown the pieces in butter and oil with a cut-up onion in a big frying pan. Pour off the fat and cook the browned chicken pieces in the liquid for ½ hour on a low flame. Add some garlic at the last. Serve it with rice.

Bailey White

P.S. I made this recipe up, and I improve it a little every time I use it.

JOSEPHINE HUMPHREYS

won the 1985 Ernest Hemingway Award for First Fiction with *Dreams of Sleep*. She is the author of *Rich in Love* and *The Fireman's Fair*. She lives in South Carolina.

Quick and Easy Feast for Thirty

One time back in the old days (the 1970s) I tried a recipe for a Germanic-sounding holiday dish called *Turducken*, which involved buying special scissors from a butcher and completely deboning a small chicken, a large duck, and a turkey, then stuffing an onion-garlic-parsley paste into the chicken, the chicken into the duck, and the duck into the turkey. The final product was served sliced crosswise. Total work time: 10 hours.

These days I use a variation on the original.

Turducken
>   6 chickens
>   6 whole garlic bulbs (ten cloves each)
>   6 cooking bags
>   6 cups Uncle Ben's converted rice
>   6 or more cans of black beans
>   6 heads romaine lettuce, prewashed
>   Olive oil, lemons, salt, pepper, cumin

Season chickens with salt and pepper. Stuff garlic into chickens and chickens into cooking bags. Roast in 340° oven about 2 hours. Serve with rice, beans perked up with cumin, and romaine with olive oil and lemon juice. Total work time: 6 minutes.

Josephine Humphreys

KATE WHEELER

was named a Best Young American Novelist by Granta. She is the author of *When Mountains Walked* and *Not Where I Started From,* which was a finalist for the PEN/Faulkner Award.

Aji de Gallina—**Peruvian Dish**

This is what I make for parties with dinner guests—easy and expandable.

Boil a whole chicken with veg's and herbs as for soup. Pick off meat in fine shreds, set aside. Give skin to the dog? Boil the bones in the stock till there's about a quart of nice stock. Degrease. Save the stock. Saute 3 (a lot of) onions. Add fresh, hot peppers to taste (4 to 6), orange colored ones if possible, and a little tumeric.

Add four slices of bread or two rolls soaked in milk till it's easy to disperse it.

Add half the stock and cook till thickened (half an hour).

Add 1 cup walnuts (or peanuts) chopped fine, 1 cup shredded "fresh" farmer cheese, and the chicken and the rest of the stock till you have a creamy and thick sauce.

Garnish with lots of black olives, sliced hard-boiled egg, and cilantro or parsley.

Serve over boiled potatoes and/or rice.

—*Kate Wheeler*

NATHANIEL TRIPP

was a platoon leader in Vietnam. His book *Father, Soldier, Son* was a finalist for the National Book Award. He has worked in film and television in New York. He lives in Vermont with his wife, Reeve Lindbergh. (See page 196.)

Thighs of Delight

8 to 12 chicken thighs
⅓ cup lemon juice
⅓ cup soy sauce
⅓ cup white wine
Lots of crushed fresh garlic
Some grated fresh ginger

Twenty-four hours beforehand, prepare the marinade of lemon juice, soy sauce, and wine. We like garlic and ginger too. Let the thighs marinate in the refrigerator in a shallow baking dish or pan. Turn them over in the morning. Then I just drain off the excess and broil them in the oven, crisping the skin on one side, turning them over to brown more on the underside, then turning them back until they are done, about 30 minutes. They're delicious served hot, and the juice left in the pan is excellent spooned over rice or couscous, but they really excel as leftovers, served cold as high protein snacks. They pack well in picnic baskets or lunch boxes; we often take "Thighs of Delight" with us when we go fishing or canoeing in the summer.

JOHN BERENDT

is the former editor of *New York* magazine and was a monthly columnist for *Esquire* from 1982 to 1994. He is the author of *Midnight in the Garden of Good and Evil*.

Sleepwalker's Chicken

For non-cooks like me, the wisest approach to the culinary arts is to know how to cook two or three dishes well enough that you can do them in your sleep. "Sleepwalker's Chicken" is one such dish, and it transcends the banality of its broiled-chickenness because it tastes so good.

Arrange chicken legs and thighs on a baking tin. (First, line the tin with aluminum foil to make the chore of cleaning up easier.) Slather Dijon mustard on each piece, then squeeze on lime juice, sprinkle 2 or 3 drops of Worcestershire sauce, and add salt and pepper. Crumble dried tarragon leaves on top.

Broil for about 12 minutes under moderate flame, making sure the mustard doesn't catch fire, then turn all the pieces over with a pair of tongs and once again apply the mustard and other seasonings and cook until done. The chicken will be flavorful and moist, and you will have a quantity of rich brown pan gravy that you can further enhance by stirring in a dollop of yogurt before you pour it over spiral pasta.

RICK BASS

is the author of seventeen books, including *Colter: The True Story of the Best Dog I Ever Had, The Book of Yaak, The Lost Grizzlies,* and *The Hermit's Story.* He lives in the Yaak Valley of Montana with his wife and two daughters.

Elizabeth's Jalapeño Chicken and Dumplings

1 whole chicken, cut up
2 cloves garlic, chopped
2 tablespoons fresh cilantro, chopped
2 slices fresh ginger root, 1 inch long
2 to 3 jalapeño peppers
3 tablespoons chopped celery
2 green onions, chopped
10 37¢ stamps

Cover chicken with water in large pot. Add all ingredients and bring to boil. Cook 'til chicken is tender and done thoroughly. (For milder stock, set jalapeños aside while boiling, returning them when cooking at lower temperature).

Strain; remove meat from bone, discarding skin, bone, and ginger slices. Chop meat into small chunks and return to stock. Bring to a low boil and add dumpings.

Dumplings
   3 tablespoons shortening
   1 ½ cups flour
   2 teaspoons baking powder
   ¾ teaspoon salt
   ½ cup buttermilk
   ¼ cup milk
   Pinch sugar

Combine ingredients in bowl. Roll out as for pie crust. Cut into 1-inch squares, keeping dusted with flour. Add one at a time to simmering stock. Cook 10 minutes uncovered, then 10 minutes covered.

This is a recipe, the chicken part of which was given to us by our friends Steve and Jamie Potenberg, and the dumpling part of which was added by Elizabeth. It goes good with or without an awful lot of white wine. It's great when you're really starving and just want to gorge. It's a great way to put a bit of strength back in your diet and to store up reserves in case you are planning, say, to expend a lot of energy writing letters to Congress, telling them to protect the vast federal wildlands of Yaak Valley, Montana, up on the Idaho, Montana, and Canadian border. Despite being the wildest valley in the Lower Forty-eight (here comes the eco-rant), Yaak still doesn't have one single acre of designated wilderness. Yaak is the "straw" going into Canada's great reservoir of wildness—over a million acres of roadlessness, just across the line—and Yaak is one of the avenues, the corridors, for the genetic dispersal (and you just wanted a recipe) of not just wolves and grizzlies into the Rockies, but elk, wolverines, lynx, and woodland caribou. Without wilderness protection for this wild valley, all of the West will become less wild, more fragmented, isolated, and ultimately sterile. The Glacier country by itself isn't enough to do it on its own—we need an optional corridor for the shyer, more secretive, deep-woods-loving populations and individuals to choose from, especially with the development that is occurring in the Flathead Valley, south of Glacier. And Congress isn't going to do this on their own.

It's really very simple. Write the Gang of Ten. You can just send each of them a copy of one letter—and tell them you want maximum protection of Yaak's federal wildlands, so that wildness can keep being breathed into the rest of the West. Yaak is down to single- or double-digit populations for so many of its endangered species: nine or ten grizzlies, four or five passing-through wolves, one or two caribou, fifteen or twenty bull trout. . . . And still, not one acre has ever been protected.

Maybe if every time we hear the word "chicken," we write the U.S. Forest Service, then we can save this valley, which has no equal. It combines the wet, lush, generous Pacific Northwest ecosystem with the harsher, more mountainous system of the northern Rockies. It is a foundation, a cornerstone, of the American Northern Rockies, and still, after all these years, it has not a single acre of protected wilderness.

Dennis Rehberg
U.S. House
Washington, DC 20515

Max Baucus
U.S. Senate
Washington, DC 20510

Dale Bosworth
Chief of the U.S. Forest Service
Box 96090
Washington, DC 20090

Conrad Burns
U.S. Senate
Washington, DC 20510

George W. Bush
The White House
1600 Pensylvania Ave.
Washington, DC 20500

Trent Lott
U.S. Senate
Washington, DC 20510

Bob Castaneda, Forest Supervisor
Kootenai National Forest
1102 Highway 2 West
Libby, MT 59923

Joe Krueger, Forest Planner
Kootenai National Forest
1102 Highway 2 West
Libby, MT 59923

Yaak Valley Forest Council
(Pro-roadless Group)
155 Riverview
Troy, MT 59935

Brad Powell, Regional Forester
Box 7669
Missoula, MT 59807

DAVID MADDEN

has published nine novels and two collections of stories, including *Cassandra Singing, Bijou,* and *Pleasure Dome.* His novels *Sharpshooter* and *The Suicide's Wife* were nominated for the Pulitzer Prize. He has taught creative writing at Louisiana State University since 1968.

Gran'maw's Chicken Biscuit Dumplings

"Honey, did I ever tell you the story of the old mountain man who took the money his wife had saved for the children's Christmas play pretties and—Oh, I bet I've boiled that hen to death!"

I sat at the big round table, enjoying once again the sight of my gran'maw fixing Sunday dinner and the sound of her voice telling stories, as she usually did when she had an audience for her cooking.

"No, gran'maw, you never did." She hoped I'd lie.

The chicken that she had killed herself, ringing its neck way out by the garden, was fine. So she checked the biscuits (made with lard). "Done and done."

"Now!" Gran'maw was part Cherokee, and they always used that word when they started to talk. "Way it was, the mother had saved up ever red cent all year long because the poor little youn'uns ain't never had no play pretties at Christmas. So down the mountain the old man went, into Elizabethton. Honey, did you scrap them carrots yet?" She had dumped the celery and onions in with the chicken half an hour before.

I shoved the bowl of skinned and chopped carrots across the table and she dumped them in the pot.

"Well, sir, come dark, the mother and the youn'uns commenced to listen real sharp. And oh, the wind set up such a commotion that ever few d'recklies they all thought they heard the old man acoming, but no. . . . Push them peas over." I pushed the bowl of peas I had shelled. Everything in that pot, smelling so good and purring at a boil, was out of her garden.

"And then what?"

"Well, it's the eggs next." She was messing with me. She took the eggs out of the icebox, stirred up the fire under the back lid, and set them to boiling beside the chicken pot.

"Now where was I?"

"You were putting the eggs on." I liked to mess with her, too.

"Being smart-mouthed around me don't play, mister. But you've heard this ol' story a hundred times and more anyway."

"I've eaten your chicken biscuit dumplings before, too, so tell it again."

"Well, sir, they was, as the man says, listening close as chiggers, when it was either him or the wind amaking a creaky wagon-wheel sound that got clos'ter and clos'ter until there it was, stopping right outside the cabin door. And, don't you know them youn'uns was thrilled to pieces? They run out, the mother coming up behind them, grinning to beat the band. So hap-py."

The phone, as if part of her act, rang. She told momma to shake a leg and get down there with the cream for the ho'made ice cream because the dinner was about cooked to death. But she kept me waiting, telling momma over and over a story about what her neighbor did to his dog. Coming back into the kitchen, she held up a finger for me to hold on, and she sheered the boiled eggs into the chicken pot and very gently blended them in with a wooden spoon.

"The mother said, 'Well, where's the children's play pretties?' And the old man said—Let me stir in the flour first. I can't concentrate on two things at onc't." The broth got thick. "Now the biscuits." She cut them in two and gently stirred them in.

"And the old man said, 'Why, woman, I got down there in Elizabethton and I got to thinking that you and me ain't got no tombstones. Help me get 'em down out of the wagon.' The mother got the red ass and said, 'You get down on the ground and I'll get up in the wagon and push 'em down to you.'"

Gran'maw set the pot over on the cooler side of the cook stove. "Now, there!"

And that's how my grandmother Merritt taught me not only how to cook but how to tell stories, too.

David Madden

BARBARA BUSH

Biographical statement, p. 34.

Barbequed Chicken

Serves 4

Marinade
    1 3-lb. fryer, quartered
    1 large garlic clove, crushed
    1 teaspoon salt
    ½ teaspoon freshly ground pepper
    1 tablespoon oil
    3 tablespoons lemon juice

Put ingredients in a heavy zip-lock bag. Shake to coat well. Refrigerate for 24 hours if possible, turning the bag several times. When coals are ready, place chicken on the grill, skin side up, basting with the marinade. Cook until well browned before turning. (If baking in oven, bake at 400°, skin side down first.) About 20 minutes before chicken is done, begin using your favorite bottled barbeque sauce or the homemade version, as follows.

Barbeque Sauce
    ¼ cup cider vinegar
    2 ¼ cups water
    ¾ cup sugar
    1 stick butter or margarine
    ⅓ cup yellow mustard
    2 onions, coarsely chopped
    ½ teaspoon each salt and pepper

Bring to a boil, cook on low 20 minutes or until onion is tender. Then add the following:

    ½ cup Worcestershire sauce
    2 ½ cups catsup
    6 to 8 tablespoons lemon juice
    Cayenne pepper to taste

Simmer slowly for 45 minutes. Taste for seasoning. This sauce freezes well.

Barbara Bush

JERE HOAR

has hunted quail with English Setter gun dogs from his own "line" and kennel for forty-five years. A former teacher, journalist, and lawyer, he is the author of *Body Parts,* a short story collection (NYTBR Notable Book), and a novel, *The Hit.*

Roast Quail

    4 quail
    4 slices bacon
    1 tablespoon butter
    ½ cup hot water
    Juice of ½ lemon
    3 ounce can of mushrooms

Wipe birds dry. Bind each in a slice of bacon. Roast birds 35 minutes, or until tender, at 350° in a buttered, black iron skillet. Then broil 3 minutes, or until bacon is done. Remove wrapped birds to a heated container. Add butter, water, mushrooms, and lemon juice to skillet drippings. Stir to make gravy. Serve birds on toast with gravy poured over birds and toast.

Jere Hoar

STEVE YARBROUGH

is the author of the novels *Visible Spirits* and *The Oxygen Man,* and three collections of short stories. A Mississippi native, he divides his time between Fresno, California, and Krakow, Poland.

Roasted, Not Caressed, Polish Duck

My wife, Ewa, is from Poland, so when I met her, back in 1984, my taste in food underwent a revolution. Some of what she fed me—red borscht, for instance, which first looked to me like a bowlful of blood—took a while to get used to. But others I fell in love with right from the start, and one of them that struck my fancy is roast duck with apples, which Ewa's father, Zygmunt, had taught her to cook. I need to say right off, though, that the ducks you get in Poland are about twice the size of the ones you get here, and this recipe is the one we use when we are in Krakow, where we live during the summer. So what I'd suggest doing is to just double everything. One Polish duck will feed a family of four, but one American duck won't, unless you're dealing with some skimpy appetites.

You need a duck, some salt, 3 or 4 medium green apples, and about 1 tablespoon of marjoram. A few hours before you start cooking, salt the duck and rub it inside and out with half of the marjoram. Cut the apples up into small slices or wedges. Sprinkle the remaining marjoram over the apples. Push the sliced apples into the body cavity and put the duck in a roasting pan. Close the body cavity (metal skewers work nicely, though in Poland we would probably sew the cavity shut). Roast the duck for 1 ½ to 2 hours, depending on weight. If the duck is particularly fatty—which most American ducks won't be—it's a good idea to make small cuts in it after 30 or 40 minutes to release a little of the fat. The duck tastes great accompanied by either stewed red cabbage or beets.

A few years ago, when my Polish was even worse than it is now, I was having dinner in a Warsaw restaurant with Ewa and the Polish novelist Piotr Szewc. I'd gotten tired of having people order my meals for me—back then Polish restaurants tended not to have English-language menus available, though most good ones do now—and in an effort to assert myself, I told Ewa and Piotr that I didn't need any help. When the waitress came to take our orders, I attempted to get the roast duck. "Kaczka pieszczona," I blithely said, prompting the waitress to burst out laughing. Rather than roast duck, I had asked for caressed duck.

JOHN DUFRESNE

is the author of *Louisiana Power and Light* and *Deep in the Shade of Paradise*. He lives in Dania Beach, Florida.

Cajun Possum Ravioli

Let me say, first of all, I don't hunt, and possum's hard to find in a supermarket. Decent road kill is easier to come by in Louisiana than it is in South Florida. Too much traffic down here. By the time you come upon a possum, raccoon, or squirrel, it's generally flattened. Even the vultures can't pry it off the tarmac. But back when I lived in Ouachita Parish, Louisiana, my friend Kebo Haley and I would go road harvesting at sunup—usually out on Highway 34 between Bawcomville and Eros or down 557 toward Luna. Most critters are killed at night, and you want to arrive at the scene of the crime before the other scavengers have had a go at the carcass.

You'll want a cooler, a bag of ice, a pocket knife, two-quart resealable plastic bags. Road kill animals enjoyed grass, trees, streams, and lived natural life before they were killed. Their flesh is natural, organic, pesticide-free. (Of course, there was that final moment when the headlights caught its eyes, and the adrenalin shot through every muscle in its tiny body.)

Carry the carcass to the side of the road. Make a cut from the anus to the ribs and remove the entrails. You might want to wear surgical gloves. (You could wait till you get home before skinning, but Kebo liked to do the whole job on the spot. The longer you wait to clean an animal carcass, the gamier the taste.) Make a slit along the center back. Insert your fingers and pull the skin in opposite directions. Possum is harder to skin than rabbit or squirrel. You might need to cut the skin up each leg to the foot, then cut the skin around the base of each foot and around the neck, pull the skin loose from the legs first, then the neck, and then the back. Wipe the carcass with a damp cloth and remove hair and debris. Remove the head, feet, tail, and excess fat. Remove the musk glands from under the front legs. Leave them for the crows and vultures. Pack your possum in the plastic bag and put on ice. When you get home, soak the possum in a salt solution overnight in the fridge.

Debone the possum and pass the meat through the fine blade of a meat grinder. Saute the meat in bacon fat, onions, and garlic. Add chopped spinach. Season to taste with salt, pepper, Tabasco, paprika, basil. Set aside in the fridge while you make the raviolis.

You'll want 2 ½ cups of unbleached flour, ½ cup of semolina flour, 4 eggs, and a teaspoon of salt. Combine the flours and salt and mound on the counter. Make a well (fontana) in the mound with your fist and crack the eggs into the center, beat with a fork to break the yolks. Work the flour into the eggs and keep kneading. Separate into four dough balls. Roll out one ball into a 12-by-10-inch rectangle and then score six rows of five 2-inch squares with your knife. In the center of each square place a small amount of your possum filling. Then cover with a second sheet of dough, using the same squaring method. Press down between the rows to create a seal. Repeat with the other two dough balls. Cook in boiling salted water for 4 minutes. Serve with a Tabasco marinara sauce.

WILLIAM HARRISON

is the author of ten books of fiction, some essays and screenplays. His last two books are *The Buddha in Malibu,* a collection of short stories, and *The Blood Latitudes,* a novel. He lives in Fayetteville, Arkansas.

Timber Rattler Stew

Locating Good Ingredients
A big fat rattlesnake is required.

This cannot be accomplished in California, where the common black rattler is thin and stringy and usually lolls around near the beach where it doesn't even bother to rattle. The best specimens range from Texas throughout the South. Diamondbacks are often more than adequate—they plump up in the summers—but a fat timber rattler fed on baby rabbits really takes a good marinade.

In Arkansas, where I've spent a pleasant exile from Texas, I found a specimen near my favorite trout river, so I invited my lunch cronies—Roy, Dr. Bill, Mort, Jack, Gerald, and Big John—to go for rattler stew. These are guys who eat quantities of cream gravy and who enjoy finding large chunks of unidentifiable meat underneath it, but a stew sounded hearty enough to them.

Killing the Snake
We made a fire near the boulders where I had often spotted my rattler. I turned over just three stones before locating him again. My pals became uneasy with this big five-footer in our midst, but I served drinks and they soon returned to their anecdotes. With my old Randall knife I cut off a sturdy branch of maple and soon began switching the snake with it. The rattler's tongue flitted out, its tail was up high and rattling away, its neck arched up ready for a strike, but I just kept switching it. By the way, a good hardwood limb is essential. Pine switches are too gentle and just won't do.

No rattlesnake enjoys a good switching. It stays mad and tries to escape, but finally gets its head down. When this happens, step on the head—as I did that evening—and cut it off. Thick shoes or boots are best in this maneuver, so again this preparation of the main ingredient doesn't work all that well in California, where the natives wear sneakers, sandals, or no shoes at all.

Be sure not to cut off too much good meat behind the head.

Preparation and Cooking

Skin the snake and throw away the rattlers.

Cut the snake lengthwise and open it as a thick filet.

Remove any dark or ugly parts.

Take your same sharp knife and give the filet about a hundred cuts. Fill the cuts with tequila. Add Worcestershire sauce for color and a dash of flavor. (Bourbon or even grain alcohol is sometimes preferred in the Deep South. There is no accounting for taste. My pal Jack wanted to use a very dry martini.)

Time must pass. Serve another round of drinks. My cronies also enjoy Ritz crackers adorned with canned cheese dip.

Make a marinade with 2 diced onions, cooking oil, another dash of tequila, a clove of garlic, a large grated carrot, a rib of diced celery, a bay leaf, salt, pepper, 1 or 2 jalapeños, and a sprinkle of coarse parsley. No mushrooms. Saute all this and when it boils get it over to the edge of the fire and let it simmer.

More time must pass. In the next hour kid around about how to add the venom. Meanwhile, cut up chunks of red potatoes, carrots, and onion quarters.

Now cut up your rattler into chunks the size of your thumb. Saute the pieces in a little cooking oil, butter, and a dusting of flour.

Simultaneously boil your vegetables, adding the marinade, a pint of water, and more tequila to taste.

Offer your pals a piece of the rattler as an appetizer.

Throw in the seared chunks of meat.

Cook until the potatoes soften.

Ask if anyone wants the severed head in his dish.

T. C. BOYLE

is the PEN/Faulkner award-winning author of ten books, including *Water Music*, *The Road to Wellville*, and *The Tortilla Curtain*, winner of the Prix Medicis Etranger.

Baked Camel (Stuffed) from *Water Music*

One evening Mungo witnessed a wedding. It was strikingly similar to the funeral he'd attended: keening hags, howling dogs, a solemn procession. The bride was a walking shroud, veiled from head to foot, even her eyes invisible. He wondered how she was able to see where she was going. The keening women followed her, their stride measured by the beat of a tabala. The groom wore slippers with upturned toes. He was accompanied by a retinue of Mussulmen in embroidered burnooses and a cordon of slaves leading goats and bullocks, and carrying a tent. At an appointed spot the tent was struck, the goats and bullocks slaughtered, a fire ignited in a depression in the earth. There was a feast. Beef and mutton, songbirds, roasted larvae and other delicacies. There was dancing, songs were sung and tales told. And then there was the pièce de résistance: a whole baked camel.

    500 dates
    200 plover eggs
    20 2-lb. carp
    4 bustards, cleaned and plucked
    2 sheep
    1 large camel
    Seasonings

Dig trench. Reduce inferno to hot coals, 3 feet in depth. Separately hard-cook eggs. Scale carp and stuff with shelled eggs and dates. Season bustards and stuff with stuffed carp. Stuff stuffed bustards into sheep and stuffed sheep into camel. Singe camel. Then wrap in leaves of doum palm and bury in pit. Bake 2 days. Serve with rice.

    Serves 400.

WILLIAM T. VOLLMANN

won the PEN/Center USA West Award for Fiction for *The Atlas*. His works include *Argall: The True Story of Pocahontas and Captain John Smith* and *The Royal Family*.

Caribou, Arctic Canada Style

1. Kill a caribou, butcher it, and cut the meat into handy 5- or 10-pound chunks.
2. Freeze until needed.
3. Take a hunk of the raw frozen meat and put it on a piece of cardboard on the kitchen floor.
4. Kneel down and chop off a handful of flakes and splinters, using a nice sharp hatchet.
5. Dip in *inukpo* (seal fat, frozen to the consistency of jelly).
6. Eat.

William T. Vollmann

THOM JONES

is a professor at the University of Iowa. His work includes *Cold Soup, The Pugilist at Rest,* a National Book Award finalist, and *Sonny Liston Was a Friend of Mine.* He lives with his wife and daughter in Olympia, Washington.

Hartebeast a'l'Africain

Directions: Knock off its horns, wipe its arse, and bung it on the plate, sport!

Kangaroo Ham

Directions: Take a chainsaw and remove the lower quadrants of your animal. (Take care when cutting the Achilles' tendons as they can snap with explosive force.) Skin, and baste the meat with a sardine liqueur. Roast lightly over a bush fire. Served with turnips, kangaroo ham is a delicious main course. Leftovers are a favorite for luncheon sandwiches, and the shank bones are wonderful for soup base, or can make a dandy, calcium-rich treat for Fido.

LARRY BROWN

has twice received the Southern Book Critics Award for Fiction and the Lila Wallace–Reader's Digest Writer's Award. His books include *Facing the Music, On Fire, Fay, Dirty Work,* and *Big, Bad Love.* He lives in Yocona, Mississippi.

Squirrel and Biscuits and Gravy

Go out into the woods, early or late, but preferably not in the middle of the day. Walk softly. You should have a gun of some sort, something like a 12-gauge shotgun with high brass #6s. Find a secluded hollow of leafy trees such as hickory, red oak, or white oak. Be quiet. Sit down. Don't talk or smoke or move, even if your ass goes to sleep. You might have to wait for a long time, especially if you made a bunch of noise coming in.

If you see a squirrel far off, don't go chasing after him because he'll only run away and you'll never see him again. They're small, but they have good eyes. The best thing is to get there before daylight, when it's still good and dark, and the squirrels are asleep in their nests, and be there waiting for them when they wake up and start feeding. You'll be able to recognize this when the limbs start jumping and moving. Be patient. Wait for them to come to you. If one comes close enough, shoot it. But don't get up and go get it. Just let it stay there, unless you've only wounded it and it starts trying to crawl off, at which point you'll be forced to go in after it and polish it off with another shot, or maybe even a stick. One good whack over the head is usually enough, and it keeps meat mutilation to a minimum.

Don't try to pick him up unless you're sure he's dead. Squirrels are small, sure, but remember that they cut those tough walnuts and hickory nuts open with their teeth, and think about what they could do to one of your fingers.

Okay. You've got your squirrel, he's dead, and you've got him in your game bag and are headed back to the house with him. The next thing you're going to need is somebody to help you dress him, unless you've been dressing them since you were fourteen and can do it by yourself.

The main idea is to get the hair off him without getting hair all over the meat because it's almost impossible to pick it off.

When you've found a willing partner, and a sharp knife, hold the squirrel between you. Pinch up a bit of the skin on his back and hold it tight between you and your partner. Slice a little hole in there, straight down. Now work your fingers into that little hole and widen it, and pull against each other. If the squirrel's not thirty years old and white around the muzzle with age, the skin should part. Just keep pulling on it until it strips off all the way around except for a tough little piece of skin that'll be on the belly. You'll have to cut through that little strip with your knife. Then work the skin on back, off the hips and the shoulders, then stop a minute. Work each of the legs out like taking a tight glove off, and cut off the feet, the tail, and the head. Cut him open from stem to stern and take out all the insides. Wash him good under the faucet, and then take him inside. He'll be dripping bloody water. Expect that.

Now, depending on what kind of load you hit him with and how close he was and whether you had to shoot him again or not, he's going to have X amount of lead pellets driven into the meat and believe me, it's not going to be any fun to bite down on one of those babies with your new porcelain crown, and if you break it you're going to have to pay Hal Haney some more money. I know. I was once over in Georgia doing a gig and a lady I was staying with fed me some kind of brittle trail mix for breakfast and I wound up paying Hal a whole bunch of money to fix my tooth after it broke. So try to dig those little lead pellets out of there as best you can.

Don't get in any hurry. This squirrel's nowhere ready to eat yet. Those lead pellets will have caused some bloody spots in the meat, and there's only one way to get them out: salty water. Put him in a pan and cover him with cold water. Sprinkle a good bit of salt over each bloody spot and then put him in the refrigerator and let him stay overnight. Pour off that bloody water the next day, rinse him in some fresh water, and then you'll be ready to cut him up.

Cut off the front legs first. Cut the rib cage off just behind the last ribs and toss it. Nothing but bone on it. Not fit to eat. But the middle back part, right behind that, has a lot of meat on it, so cut that off from the back legs, and cut the pelvic bone between the back legs in two. That gives you five pieces. It's just like dressing a rabbit.

Now if a squirrel is old, he's going to be tough. Little young squirrels that you can put in your pocket can go straight into the frying pan. But if his muzzle was kind of white, or he had some white hairs on his legs, he's old, and he's going to have to be parboiled. You don't want to eat a stringy squirrel, not after you've already gone to all this trouble, bought your license, driven out to Wally World for shells, etc.

You need to parboil a tough squirrel for a couple of hours. Put him in there and just let him cook for a while. Stick a fork in there once in a while. You'll be able to tell when he's tender.

It is morally wrong to fry a squirrel in anything besides a big black iron skillet. Put you a little vegetable oil in there and let it warm up. You're gonna want to cook him at a low heat. Get you a pan of flour and sprinkle some salt and black pepper in there. Put the squirrel pieces in there and roll them around for a while. Turn on the oven. Fix you a drink. See if you can find some good music on the radio.

Cook the squirrel until it browns, turning often. It should work up a nice crispy brown crust. Get some biscuits out of the refrigerator and put them in the oven to cook about the same time you're ready to start making gravy.

Take the squirrel out of the skillet and drain it on some paper towels. Turn the heat up a little under the skillet and sprinkle a little of that flour from your pan in there and just kind of stir it around with a fork. It'll be kind of thin and soupy at first and won't look like gravy at all, but it is actually gravy in its embryonic stage. If it's way thin, put a little more flour in there. When it starts turning brown, go over to the sink and draw you a big glass of cold water.

How brown you want your gravy is up to you. Some people don't know what the hell they're doing and let it burn and get too brown and that ruins it. You want it just a nice pale brown. When it gets like that, dump that cold water in there on it and observe the transformation. I don't know what the scientific explanation for it is or what kind of a physical thing happens in the skillet, but it's something I guess about cold water hitting hot embryonic gravy. It'll get real thin all of a sudden and then almost immediately it'll start to thicken. Just keep stirring it. Add a little more water to it until you get it just like you want it.

At this point you've got two options: you can pile that squirrel back into the skillet with that gravy and clap a lid over it and let it simmer on low heat for about 30 minutes, or you can haul those biscuits that are ready by now out of the oven and fall to just like it is. Either way, your mouth'll be happy.

Larry Brown

MEATS

Alas, I rely on real cooks. I burn lump charcoal outside in my backyard,
and I grill stuff according to Pierre Franey and Patricia Wells.

— FREDERICK BUSCH

E. ANNIE PROULX

has won a Pulitzer Prize, a National Book Award, and the PEN/Faulkner Award. Her work includes *Postcards, The Shipping News, Heart Songs and Other Stories, Accordian Crimes,* and *That Old Ace in the Hole.* She lives in Centennial, Wyoming.

Bison Steak* with a Side Dish of Salsa

Make the salsa first and let it stand about 1 hour at room temperature to develop its full flavor. Don't use anything from a can, take the trouble to get fresh ingredients.

In a large glass bowl hand-chop 2 ripe meaty tomatoes (use cultivars with low water content or you risk watery salsa) and a dozen shucked fresh tomatillos, 2 or 3 cloves of crushed garlic, a large sweet onion (dice it coarsely before adding to the other ingredients or you'll be fishing out large, unchopped pieces forever), 1 or 2 jalapeño peppers or other hot peppers with good flavor, including the seeds, a small handful of fresh cilantro, kosher salt to taste. Let it stand.

Take 2 or 3 or more frozen bison steaks from the freezer and let them stand until the frost disappears from the outer surface, half an hour or 45 minutes. The inner meat will still be frozen. (Note the lack of fat and marbling and remind yourself that without this insulation bison cooks faster than beef and is dry and tough when overcooked.) While this faint thawing is going on fire up the outdoor grill or get your cast-iron frying pan plenty hot. Rub the surface of the steaks with garlic and a little pepper and coarse kosher salt. Put them on the grill or in the frying pan. A 1 ½-inch-thick steak will be done rare in about 7 to 8 minutes; medium, 10 to 12 minutes. The frozen interior will become moist and tender during the cooking process. Take great care not to stab into the meat with a fork when you turn the steak—the juices all rush out. Use a big spatula.

Serve the steaks on warm plates with a side dish of salsa for dipping and a good Italian salad made with the best olive oil you can find (the darker green oils are superior). In season fresh-picked corn on the cob ain't bad as the third food on the plate—*no butter, just*

---

*Your neighborhood meat market doesn't carry bison? Tell your butcher to get with it. Bison is leaner and more nutritious and with a richer, fuller flavor than beef, high in protein, minerals and vitamins, and low in cholesterol and fat. It's about the only kind of meat I eat these days. I buy locally or have it shipped from the RBL Bison Ranch in Clearmont, Wyoming, 307-758-4387, though they are not always prompt and one time they forgot to put in the dry ice that keeps the goods frozen. The National Bison Association in Denver (303-292-2833) can give you some advice on other sources.

salsa and meat juice. It turns out that the only two things the damn microwave ovens do well is reheat coffee and cook corn on the cob. Leave the corn unshucked and in its husk. Put 2 ears in the microwave oven, set the temperature control on 10 or high, cook for 5 minutes, remove and shuck.

E. A. Proulx

JAY MCINERNEY

is the author of the novels *Bright Lights, Big City; Ransom, Story of My Life, Bright Falls,* and *The Last of the Savages.* He lives in New York.

McInerney Blue Plate, Red Wine Special: Seared Prime Rib Eye Steak with Goose Fat Potatoes

The biggest challenge in this recipe is securing a dry, aged prime rib eye or New York strip steak, preferably cut 1 ½ inches thick. The rib eye is more tender. That's half the game. Take it out of the fridge an hour before cooking, rub both sides with a sliced garlic clove. Meantime heat oven to 500°. Heat a cast iron skillet on the highest flame possible till it's smoking, virtually glowing. Then throw on the steak. Crank your overhead fan up all the way. Cook 5 or 6 minutes on one side till severely browned, then flip it. When both sides are browned, or even blackened, throw the skillet in the oven and cook for 5 to 8 minutes, depending on thickness of steak, for rare. To test pull it out—don't forget the pot holder—and stick a metal skewer—ice pick, whatever—through the middle, horizontally. Test skewer with tongue. If the skewer is cold, the steak needs 2 more minutes. If slightly warm, the steak is rare. Warmer, medium, etc. If the skewer burns your tongue, then something's wrong with your oven or your timer and you've got well-done leather. Let it sit for at least 10 minutes to reabsorb the juices. If you wish, make a reduction, dumping out some of the fat from the pan and replacing with a cup of beef stock (or *demi glace*), a cup of red wine, and some finely minced shallots. Boil two-thirds of the liquid away. Salt and pepper to taste. If you are cooking extra steaks, don't crowd the skillet—for 4 steaks use 2 skillets. If cooking a thicker steak, you will need to increase cooking time and you will want to carve it in thin slices for your guests.

Before you even turn on the oven, peel and rinse 4 or 5 Idaho potatoes, dice them and steam for 30 to 40 minutes, testing for medium mushiness. Let them drain, drying if necessary. Heat yet another heavy, preferably iron pan or skillet over medium high flame. Spray a little Pam in the bottom and then dump in a healthy dollop of goose fat—4 or 5 tablespoons. When the oil is good and hot, squash the potatoes in to form a rough pancake. Adjust your heat higher if they are not browning after 5 minutes. (Some trial and error is unavoidable here given variations in cooking surfaces and heating elements.) Cook 10 minutes on each side, or until browned.

Serve with salad of your choice and buxom red wine, preferably one with some nice abrasive tannins still showing to saw through that meat. The steak was expensive, so don't skimp on the juice. This meal is a platform to launch a big red wine. A big Napa cabernet, a youngish Bordeaux from a ripe year like 2000, a Syrah or (as the Aussies call it) a Shiraz. Burgundy can be a stunning match, but only the big boys, premier cru and above, need apply.

Those on the Atkins diet can skip the potatoes.

ELLEN GILCHRIST

is the author of seventeen books, including *In the Land of Dreamy Dreams, Net of Jewels, The Anna Papers,* and *Victory over Japan,* which won the National Book Award. She lives in Fayetteville, Arkansas, and Ocean Springs, Mississippi.

How to Have a Small Dinner Party

I never cook anything and I don't like to cook things or clean up the mess it makes. I do, however, know how to cook several things. I know how to cook rare roast beef. You go to the grocery store and buy the most expensive rump roast you can find. You take it out of the paper and rinse it off and then put it in an old black skillet and cook it at 325° Fahrenheit for 20 minutes per pound. Don't drink martinis while you are doing this or you will forget to take it out and then you will have brisket instead of rare roast beef. While it is cooking make some grits and stir in a pound of Kraft extra sharp cheddar cheese and half a stick of butter. Put this in a casserole and cook it in a different oven at 350° Fahrenheit for about 20 to 30 minutes. Cut up some lettuce and tomatoes if they are in season, but not in the winter when you have to get those little sour hothouse tomatoes that are probably poison. Set the table. Use all the good silver and light some candles. Put some Bach on the stereo. Call the drugstore and tell them to send out the Sunday *New York Times* and a quart of chocolate ice cream in case no one wants any rare roast beef.

   Make some coffee. Bon Appetit!

JASON BERRY

received a Guggenheim Fellowship as a jazz historian. His work includes *Up from the Cradle of Jazz, Amazing Grace: With Charles Evers in Mississippi,* and a play, *Earl Long in Purgatory.* He lives in New Orleans.

Writer's Red Meat Dinner

A CD player is necessary for successful recipe.

Preparations:
Two large filets from reputable grocer or butcher
Two bottles red wine, Graysac Medoc and St. Emilion, late 90s vintage (about $15 each.)
Vidalia onions; bell pepper
Mushrooms

For salad:
One large Creole tomato.
Spinach leaves (prewashed)
LeMartinique Blue Cheese dressing.
Artichoke hearts. Croutons.
Fresh asparagus.
Lemon
Garlic
Aluminum foil
Sweet basil
Two potatoes.

How to cook:
Turn off telephone. Open Medoc.
Music on CD, *Louis Armstrong Sings Gospel, 1931–1941* (F&A 001)
Assure integrity of the wine while you roll potatoes in foil, insert in stove at 375.
Season the filets with sweet basil and light patina of Tony Chacere's Creole Seasoning.
   Cut garlic, insert slivers into the meat.
Place meat in a shallow dish. Pour Medoc on meat but don't drench it.
Let meat soak in the wine for one hour.
CD switch *Awakaabe: Music for Sanza by Francis Bebey* (OMCD 005) Listen especially to
   the ethereal pygmy yodeling.

Cut onions, mushrooms and green pepper in solid broad strips.

CD change: *Paul Simon Rhythm of the Saints.* The drumming in cut one intensifies concentration on the cuisine.

Assure stability of the Medoc with periodic personal testing.

Brown vegetables, using careful measure of Medoc to enhance character of the vegetables. Lightly season with sweet basil and garlic salt. Keep on low flame.

Open the St. Emilion. Hold Medoc in reserve if there is any left.

CD switch: *René Marie: Vertigo* (MXJ 114) Her version of "Them There Eyes" is a lush analogue to the aromatic ambience, but after fourth cut skip to number ten, an a capella version of "Dixie," probably the best recording ever made of the song—by a black lady to boot!

After 50 minutes on high temperature remove the potatoes. Spear test with fork. If hard put back in and boost flame, otherwise remove from oven but not the foil.

CD switch: *Johnny Adams: Good Morning Heartache* (Rounder 2125)

Cut lower stems off asparagus and put in pan of boiling water 3–5 minutes. Drain, squeeze lemon, butter optional.

Put the steaks in the broiler, sizzle each side 3–4 minutes for medium rare.

Serve food.

By candle light.

Eat slowly.

CD switch: *Torch Songs: Great Blues and Swing Performances 1925 to 1945* (RPCD 324, Louisiana Red Hot Records)

When done, leave everything on the table.

Dance, slowly.

Jason Berry

ELIZABETH MCCRACKEN

is the author of *The Giant's House,* which was a finalist for the National Book Award for Fiction. Her works include *Here's Your Hat, What's Your Hurry,* and *Niagara Falls All Over Again.* She lives in Somerville, Massachusetts.

Ruth Jacobson's Midwest Brisket

This is my grandmother's recipe. Many of her best dishes involved the opening of a can of something and pouring it over something else.

> 1 brisket
> 1 can of Coca-Cola
> 1/2 bottle of ketchup
> 1 package Lipton's onion soup mix

Take brisket. If you're wondering what size, I can only say, well, sort of brisket-sized. If you want to brown the brisket first, go ahead. Then put it in a large roasting pan. Pour the onion soup mix over the brisket and rub it in, the way you'd rub any spice into a roast. Lipton's onion soup mix was one of my grandmother's favorite spices, though she also liked Campbell's Italian tomato soup.

Whisk together the Coca-Cola and the half bottle of ketchup. If you want to get fancy, you can use beer instead of Coke. My grandmother always used Coke. (She also poached apples in cherry soda pop, which turned them a lovely candy red.) I don't know whether the brand of cola matters—it occurs to me that my grandmother favored Shasta pop for drinking. When I was eleven, and in Des Moines for a visit, we had a diet Shabbat meal for a group of her lady friends—and I had just memorized the blessing over the candles, and she wanted to show me off—and we served noodle kugel with a cornflake top and offered both red and white diet Shasta pop. She gave me a white cloth napkin to wrap around the cans, as if I were a fancy waiter. We both thought this was very funny.

So it might not make a difference if you used Shasta, Pepsi, or RC. Dr. Pepper is probably out of the question. Whatever you do, *don't* substitute the Lipton's onion soup mix.

Pour sauce over the brisket. Cover with foil. Cook in a 275° oven for a while. The longer you cook it, the tenderer it gets. It'll take at least 4 hours. It might take as long as 7. Keep an extra can of Coke and the rest of the ketchup, in case you need to baste. Taste it every now and then—when it's buttery soft, it's done. You can also throw in a few onions, carrots, and potatoes toward the end. Slice the brisket against the grain.

Eat it for dinner, eat it cold at midnight straight from the fridge, eat it in sandwiches.

DAVID HAYNES

was named one of Granta's Best Young American Novelists. His works include *Live at Five, Someone Elses' Mama, Heathens,* and *All American Dream Dolls.* He lives in Saint Paul, Minnesota.

Beef Stroganoff

(Serves 4 to 6)

This recipe is perfect for those times when you invite people over for dinner, but forget to cook. You can whip the whole thing up in about 30 minutes—faster if you use that nasty-tasting instant rice. It tastes great and people think you've spent all day cooking, when really what you were doing was napping, watching TV or—heaven forbid—working on your novel. This recipe is easy to multiply, modify, and it freezes well.

> About 1 lb. of sirloin steak
> About ½ lb. of those big white mushrooms (fresh)
> About 1 cup of sour cream
> A medium onion
> A couple of cloves of garlic
> About ½ cup of your favorite wine (red is best)
> Butter or oil for sauteing
> A couple of dashes of nutmeg
> Salt and pepper
> Rice

Step One: Start some rice cooking. Any kind, but I like white rice. Make a little extra because some folks like to soak up the sauce with it.

Step Two: Clean and slice the mushrooms.

Step Three: Cut up the sirloin into cubes (bigger than die, but smaller than ice cubes). Give the bone to your favorite dog.

Step Four: Chop up the onions and garlic. Saute them in a skillet in some oil or a little bit of butter until the onions are clear. (A little brown is okay, but not too much.)

Step Five: Put the beef and the saute in a Dutch oven to brown on all sides.

Step Six: Using the same skillet, saute the mushrooms in a little butter (about a tablespoon) until soft. Add them to the beef. (Dump all that good mushroom juice and butter in there.)

Step Seven: Add the sour cream and wine. (Add more or less, depending on the consistency you like. I like my stew thicker and sometimes add a little cornstarch to thicken it [mix cornstarch with water or wine first].)

Step Eight: Heat through and season with salt and pepper and a dash or 2 of nutmeg. Serve with a nice French bread and a simple green salad.

FANNIE FLAGG

Biographical statement, p. 64.

Fried Ham with Red-Eye Gravy

Slice ham about ¼ inch thick. Cook slowly in a heavy frying pan until evenly browned on both sides. Sprinkle each side lightly with sugar during cooking. Remove the ham and keep it warm, then add about ½ cup of cold water or a cup of coffee. Let it boil until gravy turns red. Blend and pour over the ham.

   Good eats!

NORMAN LOCKMAN

writes a nationally syndicated news column for the Gannett News Service. He is associate editor of the *News Journal* in Wilmington, Delaware. He won a 1984 Pulitzer Prize for special local reporting for the *Boston Globe*.

Potted Pork Loin

For those times when only the best of friends—but not more than four—are gathered in your kitchen on a wintry Sunday afternoon, sipping strong stuff, arguing about politics, football, and fashion, demanding to be fed and expecting you to send out for Chinese food or pizza. Pull out a plate of crudite (raw veggies) and dip to keep them at bay. This is the perfect time to show off. Say, casually, "I think I'll do a potted pork loin!" (The "potted" part of the name comes from the likely condition of some of the diners, not the food. The cook should not be potted because this calls for slick work with a sharp knife.) It looks hard, but it isn't, which of course is the point of this shameless exercise. It does take time though, and the right supplies.

It's fun to watch because it's messy and your friends will think you may be making a fool of yourself. They will keep asking if you have the phone numbers for quick delivery pizza and Chinese food handy in case of a pinch. Let them freshen their drinks and hunker down to heckle. Go get your old red and white striped apron (the one you use for barbecuing outdoors, or any other article of clothing that will help you concentrate) and start pulling stuff out of the fridge. Here's what you will need on hand to pull it off:

1. 1 whole pork loin, split for stuffing, about 2 to 2 ½ pounds (can be frozen)
2. A whole bulb of garlic
3. 3 medium onions
4. A handful of baby carrots or 3 big ones
5. About a yard of twine
6. Salt (kosher if possible)
7. Cayenne pepper
8. Brown sugar or black molasses
9. A deep, narrow oven-safe glass or ceramic loaf pan big enough for the meat to fit without crowding
10. A cup of flour

A. Thaw the pork (takes about 10 minutes of "defrost" in the microwave).

B. Rinse the meat and separate the 2 halves (cut it completely through if it's not)

C. Tear apart the garlic bulb and shuck the skin off about half the big cloves. Slice them.

D. Take a sharp pointed paring knife, poke it into the pork, wiggle it to one side and insert a sliver of garlic. Insert 8 slices of garlic into each slab of pork lion. If there is sliced garlic left over, save it for something else.

E. Turn over the pork pieces. Place the UNPEELED smaller garlic cloves on 1 piece of pork, then slam the other pork piece on top to make a sandwich. No need to be gentle, and the slamming is a crowd pleaser. (You've stuffed the pork loin with unpeeled garlic, which will roast to a delicious, mild, nutty-tasting pulp. Diners may peel and eat or smear it on the bread.)

F. Take the twine, tie a loop around one end of the pork loin–garlic sandwich and then wind it round and round until you reach the other end, where you tie another loop. At this point, the pork loin should be a securely tied loaf.

G. Spread the flour out on a cutting board. Wet the pork and roll it in the flour until it is covered. This is called "dredging," in case any of the smart alecks ask. Set it aside on the cutting board, flour and all.

H. Peel and chop the onions. Use a food processor if you have one. Spread the onions as the bottom layer in the loaf pan, no more than about 1 inch deep.

I. Peel and chop the carrots. Use a food processor if you have one. Spread the carrots as the second layer in the loaf pan, no more than about 1 inch deep.

J. Place the pork loin on top of the onion and carrot layers.

K. Sprinkle water on the pork loin (a spray bottle is handiest).

L. Sprinkle the pork loin generously with about a quarter cup of brown sugar or the same amount of black molasses.

M. Sprinkle the pork loin with about a half teaspoon of salt.

N. Sprinkle the pork loin with just enough cayenne pepper to see, maybe ⅛ teaspoon (if there is such a thing). About 4 pinches is my measure.

O. Put in an oven preheated to 300° (F) for about 1 hour and 15 minutes. Do not disturb it or open the oven during this period.

P. Set the timer and restart the group argument. This time you won't need to shout because your stature will have risen considerably. Miracle workers don't need to shout.

Q. CLEAN UP!

R. Now you can have a martini.

When it is done (your guests will have long since begun to swoon over the aroma), let it rest (that's kitchen snob talk for "let it cool down a bit") for 15 minutes. Put the meat on a platter that catches the juices and slice it diagonally. Get rid of the string. Scoop out the cooked onions and carrots and heap the mixture around the sliced meat. Let it mix with the meat juices and let your guests take what they want.

Serves six.

If you've never done this, the prep time takes about a half-hour. You can get it down to 15 minutes when you've done it a few times. The cooking and resting takes another hour and a half. We're talking 2 hours total, three-quarters of which you will be free to hobnob with your starving friends.

The onions and carrots mixture works as one vegetable, but you probably ought to serve one other simple vegetable side dish, like plain ordinary peas. You may want to use frozen peas. I use canned baby peas because that's what my mommy used.

Your friends will never top this dish without professional help.

JANE MULLEN

is the author of a short story collection, *A Complicated Situation.* Her work has appeared in *Mademoiselle,* the *Oxford-American, Prairie Schooner,* and many other periodicals. She divides her time between Oxford, Mississippi, and Skibbereen, Ireland.

Sausages, Potatoes, and Apples

This is a great comfort food for a cold winter night, or a summer night in Ireland, and always gets raves. We just call it Sausages, Potatoes, and Apples.

> 6 potatoes (1 and ½ lbs.)
> 1 lb. fresh pork link sausage
> 2 tablespoons olive oil
> 2 tablespoons butter
> 2 red onions, sliced thin
> 2 Granny Smith apples
> 1 teaspoon sweet paprika
> Fresh grated nutmeg
> Minced parsley
> 1 cup crème fraiche* (or heavy cream)

Cut potatoes into ¼-inch rounds and blanch them in a kettle of boiling water for 5 to 7 minute, drain. In a large skillet, cook sausages in oil for 5 minutes, until done. Keep them warm. Discard all but 2 tablespoons of fat from skillet, add butter and cook the onions over moderate heat, stirring, for 5 minutes. Add the potatoes, the 2 apples (cored and cut into ¼-inch rounds), and the paprika and some nutmeg. Cook another 5 minutes. Add crème fraiche, bring to a boil, 2 minutes, until slightly thickened. Add sausages to warm and pile it all onto a platter.

Serves 4.

*It's a cinch to make your own creme fraiche. Just mix ½ cup of sour cream with ½ cup of heavy cream, stir together, cover, and leave at room temperature for 24 hours. Then store in fridge. Obviously, this makes 1 cup.

PADGETT POWELL

Biographical statement, p. 72.

Cracker-Yucatan Ribs

This is a heretical paraphrase of Diana Kennedy's *Cochinita Pibil* recipe in her *Cuisines of Mexico*. Her recipe is for pork loin wrapped in banana leaves and cooked underground. It takes more nerve than I have to put a good piece of meat in a hole in the ground.

You are going to make a paste, or a loose sauce, whatever you prefer, of the following seasonings in either vinegar or orange juice or both. The original recipe calls for Seville oranges—any that are sour will do. I just go with white vinegar; I do not like the wine or other fancy tinctures.

¼ to ½ teaspoon allspice
¼ to ½ teaspoon cumin
1 teaspoon oregano
3 teaspoons salt
Garlic, handful of peeled cloves
2 dozen black peppercorns
Several dried red peppers
Paprika for color, mostly

Blend these with just enough vinegar to make a heavy sauce. The figures given are very loose guides and should be regarded so. Use any ratio of this to that you like, and you needn't use all the ingredients. The essence here is conveyed, I believe, by the cumin, allspice, and salt. Marinate the slab of ribs—overnight is good, a couple of hours will do.

Ribs in black joints in Memphis may, but ribs do not to my mind need long, or particularly slow, cooking. And they can take some heat. A wood fire just hot enough to not burn them is good (with the ribs about a foot above the fire); about an hour will do, then gentle holding. You can wet the ribs with the paste/sauce as you turn them. You are basically trying to get the fat out of them, which you will never do, which is why they are good no matter what you put on them.

CLYDE EDGERTON

is the author of *Raney, The Floatplane Notebooks, Walking across Egypt, Killer Diller,* and *In Memory of Junior.* He lives in Chapel Hill and has taught at several southern colleges, including Duke University.

99.5% Fat-Free Simulated Pork Barbeque

I once invented the following recipe, then after a month or so got tired of it and forgot it. That was ten years ago. Recently I talked to a couple who told me they ate my invention all the time. It's an important recipe if you're weight conscious, but it makes no sense unless you like North Carolina pork barbeque, chopped style. It's called 99.5% Fat-Free Simulated Pork Barbeque. It has the exact texture of pork barbeque and tastes the same if you ate the pork barbeque when you had a bad cold.

    1 can tuna in spring water
    1 jar of your favorite barbeque sauce
    Hamburger buns

Put the tuna without water in a bowl, add barbeque sauce to taste, mix; then place simulated pork barbeque on the bun. Slaw is optional. It is good served with most drinks other than champagne.

PINCKNEY BENEDICT

is a native West Virginian and the author of *Town Smokes, Dogs of God,* and a collection of short stories, *The Wrecking Yard.* He is a commentator on National Public Radio's *All Things Considered* and an associate professor of English at Hope College in Holland, Michigan.

My Great-Uncle Hunter Bean's Scrapple

Salt and pepper
Powdered herbs and spices
Cornmeal
Buckwheat flour
A good big hog's head

First, you got to kill your hog.

Do not let another do the killing for you. Wielding the knife while the hog dies (and hogs die hard) will inspire you to hold your own life that much dearer. (Did you know that the louder the hog hollers as he dies, the better his meat will taste? It's so.)

Separate the head from the rest. (Use a good heavy well-sharpened meat cleaver to get you through the spine. Failing that, a decent camp hatchet will suffice.) Dispose of the other parts of the hog. (Do this as you see fit: bacon, sausage, ham, pork chops, pickled pig's feet—though every cookbook recipe for pig's feet that I know of calls for six pig's feet. Six! How does a person come by such a number of pig's feet, do you suppose? Put hog number two on crutches for a while?)

Scrape and clean the hog's head. Split the skull. (Use whatever implement you used to detach the head for this work. Split the skull in a single two-handed stroke sharp between the eyes. Do not make a mess of it.) Take out the eyeballs and the brain. The brain can make for good eating but not in this recipe. I have heard they eat the eyeballs in other nations but we do not eat the eyes here.

Scrape and clean the ears. Leave no bristles on the ears, this is vitally important! Boil water in a sizable pot, one large enough to submerge the entire head in. A big black pot works best. Simmer the head for 6 to 8 hours. By this time the meat will slip from the bones like a fine lady's silk dress glove from its owner's beautiful slender fingers.

Lift out the meat and the bones into a colander. Remove the bones and dispose of them as you see fit. Remember, a good dog loves a hog jaw. Chop the meat very fine. The fineness of your chopping now will determine the quality of your breakfast later, so do not stint in the effort!

At this stage, some of your finer folks will skim off the layer of golden grease from the water in the pot. Leave the grease on there. It will not harm you and it will sweeten the scrapple.

Return the meat to the boiling stock. Season highly. (This is where your salt and your stout black pepper, your powdered herbs and spices—your marjoram and basil and thyme and sage and tarragon and rosemary and oregano, your cumin and cardamom, and yes! even just a little pinch of cinnamon, though too much of this will spoil your scrapple beyond recovery—all these come into it right here. Do not be shy about the use of these ingredients, with the exception of the cinnamon.)

Add equal measures of fine-ground cornmeal and buckwheat flour to the seasoned stock, enough to make of it a soft mush. Stir the mush constantly. Do not allow it to stick to the bottom of the pan! Do not allow it to burn! Use some elbow grease as you stir. Do not slacken.

After a quarter to a half hour of stirring, drop the heat back. Cook the mush for an hour, a little more if it was truly a big hog's head, much bigger than your own for instance, a little less if it was smaller. Pour it into bread pans and allow it to cool. It should set nicely. Put it in the springhouse, where it is cool enough that the scrapple will keep until you have a taste for it.

Slice the scrapple. Eat it cold, by itself or on bread. Use it to soak up the yolks of your fried eggs. Do not be shy about eating it, as it is one of the best things there is to eat. Fry it for breakfast, but do not fry it hard. Make the outside crisp, but leave the insides cool and smooth. Spread on some thick sweet dark apple butter that you have made in an iron cauldron on a fire under the spreading hundred-year-old maple in your own back yard. Now there is a flavor for you!

JOHN DUFRESNE

Biographical statement, p. 139.

Doris's Tourtiere Pie

We French-Canadians eat this pie at the holidays, especially on Reveillon (Christmas Eve), but it's good at any time of the year. This is my mother's recipe that she learned from her mother. If she wants me home, all she needs to do is tell me she's made tourtiere. Here's what you'll need:

> Dough for 2 double-crusted 9-inch pies
> 2 onions, chopped fine
> 2 tablespoons of butter
> 1 ½ lbs. lean pork (yes, lean is a relative term)
> 1 ½ lbs. lean ground beef
> 1 teaspoon cinnamon
> ½ teaspoon sage
> 1 teaspoon allspice
> Salt and pepper to taste
> 6 medium potatoes, peeled, boiled, and coarsely mashed

Preheat your oven to 350°. Line 2 pie pans with dough; refrigerate dough for top crusts. In a large skillet, saute the onions in butter (no sense worrying about your heart at this point) over medium high heat for 5 minutes, or until translucent (clear and lucid, like fine prose). Add pork, beef, and seasonings, stirring constantly until the meat browns. Drain off fat (or not). (You know the trade-off here: less fat, less taste. And weren't we just told that Dr. Atkins was right all along?) Add mashed potatoes. (Yes, this presents us with a carbohydrate problem, which is why we eat it only once a year.) (Ideally, by the way, the potatoes should be Maine potatoes—Katahdins, if you can get them—not the mass-produced, bland abomi- nations from Idaho.) Mix well. Transfer to pie pans. Cover the filling with top crusts, seal, and cut slits to vent or insert one of those cute little blackbird pie vents in the center. Bake for 30 minutes or until the crust is golden brown. Serve hot.

TOM PIAZZA

is the author of a short-story collection, *Blues and Trouble*, and *The Guide to Classic Recorded Jazz*. His novel *My Cold War* won the 2002 Pirate's Alley Faulkner Society Prize for the Novel. He has been the recipient of a James Michener Fellowship in Fiction and writes regularly about music for the *New York Times*.

Original Piazza Family Meat Sauce

In the second decade of the last century my father's parents emigrated to America from Sicily, which is more or less the Mississippi of Italy. They know what they are doing when it comes to sauce. The following recipe for meat sauce comes originally from my paternal grandmother, and was modified somewhat by my mother. This is heavy, serious sauce, almost a meal in itself. It should come with a coupon for a free angioplasty. This is not nouvelle cuisine. It is *tres vieille* cuisine.

You need to cook this in a good-sized pot (4- to 6-quart size; 6-quart is better, as it will give you more maneuvering room for stirring). And a heavier-gauge pot is to be preferred over a thin, light one. The recommended utensil for stirring is a wooden spoon.

Olive oil
Several cloves of garlic
3 small cans of imported plain Italian tomato paste (NOT tomato sauce)
1 or 2 teaspoons dried or fresh basil
4 links of Italian sweet sausage (or Italian hot sausage if you prefer)
2 pork chops, ½ lb. cubed beef, veal, other meat
1 ¼ lbs. ground beef (ground round or sirloin is best)
Salt, pepper, garlic powder
1 egg
1 teaspoon parsley
3 tablespoons Pecorino Romano cheese
½ cup Italian-style bread crumbs

First, pour enough olive oil into the pot to cover the bottom generously. Add as much garlic as you like: there is no such thing as too much garlic. In any case, no fewer than 3 cloves, sliced thin. Saute the garlic in the pot on medium heat until it turns a golden color. While you are doing this open the 3 cans of tomato paste. The use of tomato paste instead of tomato sauce is essential to this recipe's character.

When the garlic is just beginning to get golden, add the tomato paste from each small can into the pot. Stir in 3 cans of water for each can of paste. Stir in the water for each can as you go, otherwise the paste will sit in a thick glob on the bottom of the pot. Use imported plain tomato paste; my mother recommends Pope brand, and emphatically warns against any brand that calls itself "Italian style"; these often contain oregano, which many people think is the definitive Italian spice but which is really the kiss of death in Italian cooking.

With each can of paste, stir in the 3 cans of water until the mixture is smooth. Do this until 3 cans of paste and 9 cans of water are all in the pot, and smooth. If it's still too thick, you can add one more can of water, at most. Now you can add some salt, to taste, maybe a teaspoon worth, and turn the heat up under the pot until the mixture is simmering—not boiling. Small bubbles only—"smiling," my Mom says, "not laughing." As it simmers, stir it only occasionally with the wooden spoon; the rest of the time leave the spoon parked horizontally across the top of the pot, slightly to one side, with the lid propped open on it. This way some steam will escape, but the sauce won't cook down too quickly. You can also add a teaspoon or so of dried basil.

IN THE MEANTIME: in a skillet off to the side, brown 3 or 4 Italian sweet sausages (link style, not patties. You can also use Italian hot sausage.) Stab the sausages each a couple of times with a fork before cooking, so some fat drains out. (My mother drains the skillet and spoons out the excess fat as they cook.) Cook the sausages at low-medium heat until they are well browned. You can do the same thing with 1 or 2 pork chops, or chunks of beef such as stew meat. You brown this in the skillet along with the sausage and as the meat gets brown, add it slowly to the sauce.

MEATBALLS. Meatballs are an essential part of this sauce. Have a large bowl ready. Buy about 1 ¼ pounds of ground round or ground sirloin. Take a quarter to a third of this meat, without shaping it into meatballs, and put it in the skillet along with the sausage and other meat. As it browns, add it to the sauce in the pot along with the other meat; this gives the texture and flavor of ground beef to the sauce and is an important element.

Put the remaining ground beef into the large bowl. Beat 1 egg separately and add it to the beef, mashing it in with a fork; make sure to spread it evenly through the meat so that all the meat is wet. Add salt, pepper, and garlic powder. Some people add half a teaspoon of parsley and a couple tablespoons of grated parmesan or Pecorino Romano cheese, which is, according to my Mom, made with goat's milk.

Add ¼ cup of Italian-style seasoned bread crumbs to the beef-and-egg mixture, mashing it in with a fork and then kneading it thoroughly into the beef by hand. (Progresso brand bread crumbs contain parsley and cheese and are recommended by my mother.) The fattier the ground meat, the more bread crumbs the mixture can take without getting too dry; if the mixture still seems too wet, add a small amount more of the bread crumbs.

When the bread crumbs have been well spread through the meat, you are ready to make meatballs. Take a small handful of meat out of the bowl, put it between your hands and roll it around until it turns into a ball. They should be, according to Mom Piazza, "dryish, but not too dry."

At this point I tried to pin my Mom down a little more on the specifics of the meatballs. "How dry is 'too dry'?" I asked her.

"You don't want them to fall apart," she answered.

"Okay. And how big should the meatballs be?"

"I don't know—meatball size."

"Come on," I said. "The size of a tennis ball?"

"Oh God, no. A tennis ball?"

"Well, how big?"

"I don't—maybe the size of a golf ball."

"A golf ball?" I said. "That's way too small. What are we making—Swedish meatballs? How about a raquetball?"

"No! Not a racquetball! I don't know how big a racquetball is. You don't want them to be too big," she said. "They take too long to fry and cook through. And they get unwieldy— they don't look nice. Maybe an inch and a half to two inches."

"In diameter," I added.

"Right. More than that and they're too big. They should be able to get about eight meatballs out of the mixture."

So there it is. It sounds about right to me—1 ½ to 2 inches across, and shoot to get about 8 meatballs out of the bowl.

By the time you've mashed the egg and bread crumbs into the ground beef, all the other meat (sausages, pork chops, etc.) has been transferred from the skillet into the pot and is cooking in the sauce. Drain the fat from the skillet but don't wash it out; cook the meatballs in the skillet on medium heat. As they fry, let them brown and form a little crust before you turn them, or they will fall apart when you add them to the sauce. Brown the meatballs more or less all over; when they are brown on most sides, add them carefully to the sauce in the pot and stir gently.

After the meatballs have been added, cook the sauce for 1 ½ hours at a simmering rate. If the sauce looks as if it might be getting too thick too quickly, you can add a little water. Simmer, as before, with the lid propped open by the wooden spoon. Cook this sauce very slowly, on low heat. Stir it occasionally so that things don't stick to the bottom of the pot. When the fat begins to visibly rise to the surface, the sauce is close to done.

The pasta is a matter of choice, but Mom recommends using this heavier sauce over a heavier pasta, such as rigatoni or penne, rather than spaghetti or linguini, although I have had it over spaghetti and it works just fine that way, too.

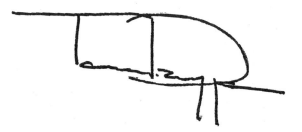

CHRIS OFFUTT

is a Guggenheim Fellow and a Granta Best Young American Novelist. He is the author of *Kentucky Straight, Out of the Woods, The Same River Twice,* and *No Heroes.* He lives in Albuquerque, New Mexico.

Kentucky Breakfast

steak
bourbon
and a dog
to eat the steak

SANDWICHES, BREADS
& ONE CHEESE PUFF

*Sadly, I have no recipes to share; my repertoire pretty much
ends with oatmeal and instant coffee.*

—TONY HORWITZ

JOHN UNDERWOOD

is an award-winning journalist and nationally-known author who has covered everything from space shots to major sporting events throughout the world. His nine books include *My Turn at Bat, Bear,* and *Tales out of School.* He lives in Miami.

The Tomato and Lettuce Sandwich

The one item that sustained me as a child and probably kept my widowed mother off the welfare rolls: The Tomato and Lettuce Sandwich.

I wrote it down for my wife, whose kitchen is festooned with the gaudiest and grandest cookbooks man has ever known, and she said it was out of the question for inclusion in a book of viable recipes. She said The Tomato and Lettuce Sandwich was "a dish made popular by the Great Depression, and therefore not something healthy appetites need to be reminded of." She said, too, that "the way you describe it makes it clear that in the wrong hands it could be a disaster. Might even get you sued."

Looking over it now, I think she has a point. For example, the only proper bread for The Lettuce and Tomato Sandwich has to be "as gummy as possible" (according to the recipe). This requires pinching the loaves at the super market until you find one that doesn't bounce back. It could get you in a lot of trouble.

Secondly, I can see a certain amount of confusion over the requirement that "the tomatoes be extremely ripe, or green, or somewhere in between." This does not confuse me, of course, because a "heavy coating of mayonnaise on each slice of bread, together with enough salt and pepper to blot out the color of the tomato" neutralizes everything and allows for latitude in shopping that takes into consideration the vicissitudes of vegetable growing.

Moreover, I told my wife, such liberality in the essential ingredient serves to recognize the botanical truth that what was once green might well, off the vine, become bloody (even slimy) red, at which time one should be prepared to make the best of things. My wife thought that was "unheard of."

She also had a few things to say about my criteria for a "serviceable piece of lettuce," more or less on the same line. As to what she said about my hints on what to look for when The Tomato and Lettuce Sandwich has been sitting in the refrigerator for four days, I would just as soon not get into it.

JOHN ED BRADLEY

was team captain of the Louisiana State University Tigers football team in 1979. He has written for the *Washington Post, Sports Illustrated,* and *Esquire* and is the author of six books, including *Tupelo Nights, Smoke,* and *My Juliet.* His latest book is *Restoration.*

Hurricane Lili Mayonnaise Sammitch, Cajun Style

I've lived through many hurricanes and so I've eaten plenty of these sandwiches. They're not that bad, but I doubt they'll ever catch on outside the Gulf Coast.

> White bread (optional)
> Crackers (optional)
> Tabasco sauce (optional)
> Family size jar of Blue Plate mayonnaise

Wait until the lights go out and tree limbs smash down on your roof. Wait until the wind blows out a couple of windows. If your flashlight isn't working, find some matches and light a candle. If the matches got wet, or if you can't locate a candle, don't worry about it. It's your trailer and you should know the layout by now.

Have a seat in the kitchen. The floor is fine. Don't be too hard on yourself. True, you might've gone to Wal-Mart for provisions such as potted meat and dried shrimp like everybody else in the parish, but it's too late to dwell on that now. Take a deep breath. Relax. Remember back to when the weather was good and the frig was full.

If you have a wife, call her in and talk about the meals you've enjoyed together. Be positive and have faith in the construction company that stapled together your double wide. Remind yourself that others along the bayou are getting hammered too. Do not swear at God, no matter how hungry you might be. Do not become amorous, either. It is important for you to save your strength. Take joy in the memory of the leftover jambalaya you had for supper last night. When your wife's stomach begins to growl, please do not mention it. Mention it and yours is likely to sympathize and growl too. This will only aggravate the situation. If you don't have a wife, spend this time with your pet. Make your peace with the animal. Promise it real food scraps if you survive.

Wait until the bayou crests and the cinder blocks beneath you collapse in the mud. Wait until you hear cows mooing as twisters lift them out of the fields and carry them away. Blue Plate mayonnaise, like all other brands of mayonnaise, is perishable. Please do not wait until the inside of the frig is warm before reaching for the jar. Go ahead and unscrew the lid now. If you don't have bread, don't worry about it. Crackers will do. If you don't have crackers, use a knife. If you don't have a knife, try a finger.

Stick it in deep and remove as much as you can. Blue Plate uses eggs to make its mayonnaise, so at least you're getting your protein. Add Tabasco to taste. Eat to your heart's content, then share what remains in the jar with your wife and/or pet.

If either complains, remind her/it that you were as surprised as anybody when Lili didn't come ashore farther to the east. If the pet barks or meows, put it outside with the flying cows. If your wife says a word, hand her the mustard and see if she can do better.

DAVE BARRY

writes a weekly nationally syndicated humor column for the *Miami Herald*. His books include *Big Trouble, Dave Barry Slept Here, Dave Barry Does Japan,* and *Dave Barry's Complete Guide to Guys.* He lives in the suburbs of Miami.

Toast with Peanut Butter

This is a hearty snack that I generally enjoy thirty or forty times per day when I'm supposed to be writing a column. You get yourself a slice of white bread, the kind with no fiber or vitamins or anything else healthy in it, and you put it in your toaster and push the lever down. I like my toast well done, so I push the lever down three or four times, until the smoke detector is beeping. Then I get a spoon and smear a fist-size gob of Peter Pan peanut butter (creamy, NOT chunky!) on the toast and eat it.

HINT: If you're in a hurry, you can skip the toast and put the peanut butter straight into your mouth. *ADDITIONAL HINT:* If you're in a *real* hurry, you can also skip the spoon.

ANN FISHER-WIRTH

is professor of English at the University of Mississippi. She is the author of *William Carlos Williams and Autobiography* and has published poems in many journals. Her first book of poetry, *Blue Window,* will be published in 2003.

The King Meets the Queen: It's Sandwich Time

So. You take you a couple them big slices Wondabread and slather em up good with peanut butter. Then you squash you 1 big banana, er you kin slice it, n lay it up top the peanut butter. Meantime you fry up 5, 6 slabs a bacon n kinda lay it out er crumple it up top a the banana. Slap them pieces a Wondabread together like you was slapping up some sense in a dumb ole hound dog. Take you 5, 6 spoons of butter n fry that sucker up good. Serve with Portabellas au Gratin overlaid in the Knights Medieval Crisscross Pattern (see Martha tape, $49.95) with sprigs of fresh rosemary and a nice dry Pouilly Fuissé in Baccarat tulip goblets, while the sun sets over the Sound and the children and retainers play bocce ball on the freshly landscaped terrazza.

Ann Fisher-Wirth

TONY HILLERMAN

is the author of fifteen novels. Winner of Edgar and Grand Master mystery awards, he is the author of *Skinwalkers, Coyote Waits, Talking God, Sacred Clowns,* and *Seldom Disappointed*. He resides in Albuquerque, New Mexico.

Salami Sandwich

My recipe:
    One (1) sheet rye bread
    One slice salami
    One teaspoon mayonnaise
    One sun-ripened, never in the frig, just picked from Marie's garden Beefsteak or
       Celebrity tomato

Spread bread lightly with mayonnaise.
Apply Salami.
Remove one 8-millimeter-thick slice from tomato.
Place slice atop salami (two slices if tomato is small).
Fold bread carefully, keeping tomato slice in proper place.
Secure napkin in left hand to remove juice from chin.
Eat.

Tony Hillerman

(Who has tested and tried above on numerous occasions.)

P. J. O'ROURKE

writes for *Rolling Stone*. His books include *Parliament of Whores, All the Trouble in the World, The Bachelor Home Companion,* and *The CEO of the Sofa.* He lives in Washington, D.C.

Bachelor Cooking

There's only one secret to bachelor cooking—not caring how it tastes. If you achieve this, everything will be fine. Bachelor cooking is a matter of attitude. If you think of it as setting fire to things and making a mess, it's fun. It's not so much fun if you think of it as dinner.

I have several specialties. Instant coffee is one. Simple omelets are another. My recipe: Add contents of refrigerator to two eggs and cook until everything stops wiggling. A bachelor friend of mine has an interesting variation. Mix last night's Chinese take-out food with your scrambled eggs. (Remove fortunes from fortune cookies first). He calls it Egg Foo Breakfast.

Many cookbooks claim their recipes are simple. But follow the instructions and the next thing you know you're up to your nose in larding needles and double boilers, trying to make béarnaise sauce with chip dip and milk out of the cat's bowl. The following recipes, however, really are simple, having met these four stern bachelor criteria:

1. Quick
2. Require ingredients you probably already have and that are definitely available at the 7-11
3. Involve foodstuffs able to withstand overcooking, undercooking, house fires, and being dropped on the floor
4. Have instructions so simple you don't have to follow them

These recipes also produce lousy results. But you can't have everything.

Real Hamburgers

The secret to getting that compelling-disgusting burger flavor that only roadside bars and all-night diners seem able to achieve is as follows:

1. Cheap ground beef that's at least 30% fat and 20% filler
2. A dirty skillet (readily available in most bachelor households)

Moosh the burger patties down flat, put a bookend or doorstop on top of it, and turn the stove flame up high so that everything gets splattered. Use heaps of salt and pepper and only the gooiest untoasted burger buns. Garnish according to how wide you can open your mouth.

To make a cheeseburger, be sure to use cheese *food,* not real cheese. Atomic breeder reactors cannot melt real cheese. Slip the cheese slice on top of the meat after the initial doorstop squashing, and cover the skillet with something (not your hand) until cheese food drips onto skillet surface and looks like coal tar. Serve with beer, chips, another hamburger, more beer.

Doggy Melt

Boil or heat a hot dog or leave it out to get warm. Put it on a piece of toast or bread with a slice of Velveeta cheese on top and put the whole thing in the oven. Doggy melts make a great plea for help. Fix these to make a woman feel sorry for you.

BERNARD MALAMUD

(1914–1986) was the author of eight novels, including *The Natural* and *The Assistant.* He won his second National Book Award and the Pulitzer Prize for his novel *The Fixer.* The following recipe was submitted by his daughter Janna Malamud Smith.

Hamburger

As to my father's cooking. He didn't. My mother, on the other hand, was and is an excellent cook. And although occasionally he hungered for the Russian Jewish cuisine of his childhood, her Italian food tended to please him.

The only time I can remember him touching a cooking implement was when my mother was temporarily down with some virus, or briefly away, and my brother and I needed dinner. Usually on such nights we headed out for a drive-in meal. But once in a while, Dad would cook us a hamburger himself. Outside the shaping of the meat into a pattie, his only gourmet twist was to spread a little mustard on the browned side after he flipped it!

—Bernard Malamud

ANNE TYLER

won the 1985 National Book Critics Circle Award for Fiction for her novel *The Accidental Tourist* and the 1988 Pulitzer Prize for *Breathing Lessons*. The author of fifteen novels, she lives in Baltimore, Maryland.

Hot Crab Sandwiches

¼ cup homemade mayonnaise
1 tablespoon minced parsley
2 tablespoons sour cream
1 ½ teaspoons fresh lemon juice
¼ teaspoon garlic salt
½ lb. fresh jumbo lump crabmeat
4 English muffins, fork-split
Butter, room temperature
8 slices Swiss cheese
Sprinkling of paprika

Combine the first 5 ingredients. Then mix in the crab, using your hands. (Sorry, it's the only respectful way to treat crab.) Spread the English muffins thinly with butter, cover with the Swiss cheese and top with the crab mixture. Dust with paprika.

Bake at 350° for 15 to 20 minutes, or till lightly browned on top. Serves 4.

SANDRA CISNEROS

is a poet and a novelist. She received the Lannan Foundation Literary Award for Fiction and the PEN Center West Award for Best Fiction in 1991 for *Woman Hollering Creek*. Her work includes *The House on Mango Street*, *My Wicked Wicked Ways*, and *Caramelo*. She lives in San Antonio, Texas.

Grandpa Cordero's Famous Tacos

My grandfather, my mother's father, survived three major wars, one in Spanish, two in English, not to mention "The Great Depression." He knew what going without was. When my grandmother died, he had to do without her too.

And so, without a wife to make his tortilla, Grandpa Cordero had to learn how to make them himself. He did. Big dusty towers of flour tortillas hot off the *comal*, the griddle. I remember sitting on newspapers in the kitchen—Why were there always newspapers on the chairs?—and Grandpa serving us hot tortillas, and the kitchen always dark, because Grandpa Cordero didn't believe in wasting electricity.

We usually ate these homemade tortillas with butter and salt. But sometimes Grandpa Cordero would get fancy. Here are two recipes I remember from that time.

Peanut Butter Tacos
You will need flour tortillas (never corn!) for this recipe—homemade is better, but store-bought is okay too. Any kind of peanut butter.

1. Heat your tortilla on a griddle, or heat in a microwave if you like it soft, or directly over the range if you prefer your tortilla a bit burnt, which is actually very tasty.
2. Spread peanut butter while tortilla is hot.
3. Fold in half.
4. Eat.
5. Say—"*¡Ay que rico!*"

Fried Bologna Tacos
    Bologna
    Flour tortillas

1. Fry bologna in a frying pan until it puffs up like little hats.
2. Place bologna on heated flour tortillas.

3. Add mustard (must be French's variety—not Grey Poupon).
4. Eat.
5. Too delicious for words.

BETH HENLEY

won the 1979 Pulitzer Prize for her play *Crimes of the Heart.* She also wrote *The Miss Firecracker Contest.* A native of Mississippi, she lives in Los Angeles.

Corn Bread Gone South of the Border

1 can cream corn
1 cup cornmeal
½ cup oil
1 cup buttermilk
½ teaspoon salt
1 large onion, chopped
2 hot peppers, chopped (add more to taste!)
2 eggs
6 ounces Longhorn-style cheese, grated

Mix and bake at 350° for 35 to 45 minutes. Bread will seem moist when done.

Beth

JAMES A. AUTRY

is the former president of the magazine group for Meredith Corporation. He is the author of seven books, including *Nights under a Tin Roof, Life after Mississippi,* and *Love and Profit: The Art of Caring Leadership.* He lives in Des Moines, Iowa.

Sam Gore's Corn Bread

Note: First thing is check to be sure that there ain't nobody coming to eat that you don't particularly like 'cause hit would be a shame for them to git aholt of any of this corn bread.

 Meal (Pine Mountain self rizin' preferred)
 Egg, lard, buttermilk, salt, skillet (iron)

Put the lard in the skillet and put it in a hot stove and while it is gitting good and hot mix the meal and salt and the egg and pour in enough buttermilk to make it kind of sloppy. Then pour in the hot lard and stir it up good and pour it back into the hot skillet.

 Bake at 475°; when corn bread is about done, brown the top under the broiler.

 Hope you remember to take the butter out to soften at the start of all this!

 Author's note: Sam Gore was an Eastern Airlines pilot at the time he wrote this recipe, having returned from 250 combat missions in Viet Nam, with a distinguished flying cross, and having resigned from the Air Force. After the ignominious destruction of Eastern Airlines by Mr. Lorenzo (the Dr. Kevorkian of the airline business), Sam returned to farming near Houston, Mississippi. In the summers, he operates small planes and a commercial fishing operation in Alaska where, it is reported, he still cooks this corn bread. Plus, he and I still play music together in a group called "The Over the Hill Jazz Band." Call us for weddings, funerals, bar mitvahs, and so on.

LOUISE SHIVERS

Biographical statement, p. 24.

Fried Corn Bread

This is the corn bread that our large (ten children) family always ate when I was growing up in eastern North Carolina. It is so good that we always preferred it to baked corn bread or hush puppies.

The secrets to the fried corn bread are the using of good meal and the shaping of the "cakes." Wet your hands each time you shape a cake. My ninety-year-old mother wrote this out just before she died.

I use "meat-grease" to fry it in. Don't put too much in the pan. Cover the bottom and as it is used up a little, more can be added if necessary. This gives the bread a good flavor. (Unless you are on a fat-free diet. We never were.)

Mix meal, a little *sprinkling* of flour, some baking powder (maybe a teaspoonful or two) and some salt—just guess at the amount. Mix with water, make into cakes, any size, drop into the grease, and just fry it.

Grease from bacon, fat back, or even sausage is fine.

JOHN T. EDGE

Biographical statement, p. 15.

Hot Water Corn Bread

Inspired by Sarah's in Ruston, Louisiana

> 1 cup white cornmeal
> 2 cups boiling water
> Salt to taste
> Red pepper to taste
> Oil for frying

Pour boiling water over salted cornmeal, stirring as you go. Pour only three-quarters of the water and stir vigorously until it starts to come away from the sides of the bowl. If you need more water to loosen the mixture somewhat, add it quickly before the water cools. You are, in essence, cooking the cornmeal.

When the cornmeal mixture is just cool enough to handle, sprinkle a bit of red pepper on the mix, grease your hands slightly, and roll the meal into cylinders. Fry in roiling oil of at least an inch in depth. Turn once.

Serve when browned with Potlikker Consommé. (See page 83.)

STEPHEN CALDWELL WRIGHT

Biographical statement, p. 36.

The Wright Corn Bread Muffins

2 cups of self-rising cornmeal
¼ cup of self-rising flour
2 eggs
Canola oil
Lawry garlic salt with parsley
Dark brown sugar
Cream
Water

Mix cornmeal, flour, and eggs (stir to even mixture). Add 1 tablespoon of canola oil and stir. Add a sprinkle of garlic salt. Add ¼ cup of brown sugar. Add cream and water until mixture is fluid for muffin pan (makes 12).

Spoon mixture into greased muffin pan (use canola oil to ensure each muffin space is properly greased).

Bake at 350° until evenly golden around edges and tops.

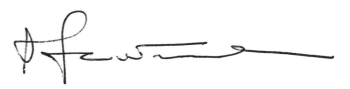

R. W. (JOHNNY) APPLE JR.

is the associate editor of the *New York Times*. In a forty-five-year journalistic career, he has written from every state in the union and 110 foreign countries, covering the Civil Rights movement, the Vietnam War, the Gulf War, and ten presidential campaigns. He lives in Washington, D.C.

Sweet Corn Fritters

Writing about food is not nearly as hard as cooking it. Despite decades of tucking in my napkin at some of the world's great restaurants, grand and much less so, and interviewing many of the world's great chefs, I remain a semi-skilled if enthusiastic amateur at the stove. But that doesn't keep me from getting my licks in, especially on weekends at our farm in Pennsylvania.

When we have guests—either our kids or friends—a gala breakfast often seems in order. Here's a favorite breakfast main dish, adapted from one served at Bill's, a cafe in Sydney, Australia, that my wife, Betsey, and I like to visit when we are travelling Down Under. It is especially good in late summer, when corn and tomatoes raised on nearby farms are bursting with ripeness.

1 cup all-purpose flour

1 teaspoon baking powder

¼ teaspoon salt

¼ teaspoon Tony Chachere's Cajun seasoning

1 tablespoon sugar

2 eggs

½ cup whole milk

2 cups corn, cut freshly from the cob (preferably Silver Queen or Golden Bantam)

½ cup diced red pepper

½ cup sliced spring onions

¼ cup chopped coriander (cilantro)

4 tablespoons vegetable oil

8 slices of bacon (from a small smokehouse, if possible)

4 medium tomatoes, sliced in half

Extra virgin olive oil

Sea salt

Freshly ground pepper
1 bunch arugula, washed and dried
Maple syrup

Preheat the oven to 350°. Put the tomatoes on a baking tray, cut side up, and sprinkle liberally with olive oil, sea salt, and pepper. Roast for 40 minutes. Meanwhile, fry the bacon until crisp, drain and keep warm.

Sift flour, baking powder, salt, and seasoning together into a large bowl, stir in sugar and make a well in the center. Combine the eggs and milk in a second bowl. Gradually add the egg mixture to the dry ingredients and whisk until you have a smooth, rather stiff, lump-free batter.

Put the corn, red pepper, onions, and coriander into a third bowl and add just enough batter to bind them lightly. Heat 2 tablespoons of oil in a large, non-stick frying pan and drop in 2 heaping tablespoons of batter per fritter, to form 4 fritters in all. Cook fritters for about 2 minutes on one side, then turn and cook slightly less on the other. They should be golden, not brown. Transfer to a warm plate while repeating the process to make 4 more.

To serve, put a fritter on each plate and top with 2 tomato halves, 2 bacon strips, and a small handful of arugula. Finish with a second fritter on top and drizzle maple syrup around the base of the stack.

Serves 4.

REEVE LINDBERGH

is the daughter of aviator-authors Charles A. and Anne Morrow Lindbergh. She is a novelist and the author of children's books. Her work includes *Under a Wing* and *No More Words: A Journal of My Mother, Anne Morrow Lindbergh*. She lives in Vermont with her husband and family. (See page 129.)

Aunt Ellie's Cheese Puff

4 cups buttered, diced bread
4 cups cheese (cheddar or other strong cheese)
2 ½ cups milk
3 to 5 eggs
Dry mustard
Salt (optional) and pepper to taste

Preheat oven to 375°.

Place in buttered casserole: one layer bread cubes, one layer cheese. Sprinkle each layer with pepper and dry mustard, salt if desired. (I omit salt, as Vermont cheddar cheese doesn't need it.) Repeat until dish is well filled, finishing with a layer of cheese.

Beat egg-milk mixture lightly, pour over all. Bake uncovered 45 minutes to 1 hour.

This recipe is for a 9-by-13-inch pan, but you can alter it—½ cup milk per egg is a good ratio.

I always make this for a monthly writers' group meeting, since it *cannot* fall like a soufflé.

Reeve Lindbergh

DESSERTS

Thank you for your invitation to include one of my
culinary delights. . . . Unfortunately, I have none.

— SCOTT TUROW

JILL MCCORKLE

is the author of five novels and three short-story collections, most recently *Creatures of Habit.* She lives with her husband and two children near Boston, where she teaches in the Bennington College Master of Fine Arts program and spends a lot of time trying to duplicate good Southern food.

Gramma's Pound Cake

One of my earliest memories in life is sitting on my grandmother's kitchen counter, feet in her deep porcelain sink, and watching her add this and that to the red polka-dotted Fire King mixing bowl which was always carefully placed under the freestanding mixer in the corner. My sister and I could not wait to lick the bowl and there was great effort—on my grandmother's part—to distribute the cake batter evenly. The batter was as good if not better than the cake. Once the bowl and all utensils were licked clean, we went back to our Saturday morning business of Sky King and Roy Rogers, knowing that in a little over an hour we would get a warm slice of the finished product, usually with a big dollop of whipped cream we had also licked up after. The cake had many lives. On birthdays, a thick creamy frosting made from powdered sugar and Crisco (always a key ingredient) decorated the surface, and in summer the abundance of North Carolina blueberries came into play. My grandmother would (last minute before baking) sift fresh blueberries (about a cup) in cake flour and then fold them into the batter. Often they would sink slowly through the rich batter to form a wonderful blueberry glaze on top of the cake. This was the version best served straight from the oven.

The Ingredients (I am told that they HAVE to be done in this order—could be a superstition but I never risk it!)

3 cups sugar

3 cups cake flour (Swan's Down the preferred brand)

1 cup Crisco (as I said, the key ingredient in anything good is always Crisco)

1 cup milk

5 eggs (these should always be whipped up in a separate bowl in case there's a bad one, so you don't waste all that sugar, flour, and Crisco)

1 stick oleo (now I have broken tradition here and also used sweet butter, which did not seem to hurt it at all)

1 pinch of salt

½ teaspoon baking powder

1 teaspoon vanilla

Bake in preheated 350° oven for 1 hour and 10 minutes. You can sing in the kitchen but you should never jump around or dance while the cake is in the oven. Because ovens vary it is important to check the status at an hour. Though I'm sure a fork would do, I was taught to check it with a toothpick, which should come out clean when the cake is done. Let cool before flipping onto a plate. I always use a pound cake pan (hole in center) which I first grease with butter and then line with waxed paper. When cool, slowly peel away the waxed paper. Warning, the top part before flipping over is the best part of all and highly addictive—I have many times picked off the whole surface without meaning to. For the birthday cake version, fill the hole with Nilla Wafers and then ice over to make a smooth surface for candles and writing!

KATE LEHRER

grew up in Texas. Her novel *Out of Eden* won the Western Heritage Award. She is also the author of *Best Intentions* and *When They Took Away the Man in the Moon.* This is her "first and probably last cookbook entry."

Mama's and Aunt Big Sister's Three-Layer Devil's Food Cake

A Kate Lehrer Disclosure

I'm sharing with you a recipe for my mother's chocolate cake, as far as I'm concerned, the best chocolate cake recipe in the world and, as far as I know, the first time it has ever been in print anywhere. Be appreciative. According to my mother, an Italian family with a small restaurant in Dallas gave their recipe to her because she loved this cake so much but asked her not to reveal the ingredients. She didn't except to her sister, my Aunt Big Sister. Years later after my aunt died, Mama, as I called my mother until I reached the sophisticated age of fourteen, passed her secret on to me. By that time I had pretty much given up on anything more elaborate for dessert than store-bought ice cream and cookies.

Unfortunately for my family, cooking never caught on with me. My children thought tuna salad two or three times a week a normal American dinner. Not that my mother didn't lecture me on preparing my husband a hot meal. And for a long time I tried, Lord, I tried.

He, however, was happier without my hot meals unless they included hamburgers or hot dogs or lasagne or his own leftover chili. (See page 95 in this book for his really, really good chili, which I always volunteered for pot luck dinners. Fearful of my botching his favorite food, he grumbled but he made it.)

Meanwhile, back to that most delicious of all cakes. I am combining Aunt Big Sister's version, which she gave to my daughter Jamie, with my mother's version given to me. They are essentially the same, but I was told to grease and flour the three round pans, as if I might not know that, and to bake at 350° about 25 minutes or until the cake shrinks from the pan when done. Just remember, the orange rind is the secret to this cake's success.

As for the icing, the cook decides. My mother and aunt had no special secrets on that score though my daughter Jamie says their icing was always made from scratch. On occasion, I have done boxed, but if I go to the trouble of making the cake, I might just as well keep trying for an icing as fudgey tasting as theirs. Am I too old to blame my mother for not giving me a really fantastic icing recipe, enabling me to make an all around perfect cake, if not myself a perfect person?

2 ½ cups sugar
1 cup butter

Cream butter and sugar well.

¼ cup warm sweet milk
2 big tablespoons cocoa

Dissolve cocoa in the milk and beat well into butter-sugar mixture.

1 cup buttermilk
1 teaspoon baking soda

Dissolve well and add to mixture.

2 ½ cups flour

Sift 10 to 15 times if it's biscuit flour.

5 eggs

Beat yolks and whites separately. Add whites last thing to mixture. (Mama's variation: beat eggs in one at a time to above mixture.)

1 grated rind of orange

Add to batter.

Then, of course, pour in 3 round (greased and floured) pans. Bake at 350° about 25 minutes. (Cake shrinks from pan when done!) (Note: my aunt didn't bother with oven heat or cooking time. She assumed everybody knows that.)

Beat batter "to death." The more you beat, the better the cake.

JACK BUTLER

is the author of the novels *Nightshade, Living in Little Rock with Miss Little Rock,* and *Jujitsu for Christ.* He won the 1978 Black Warrior Review first prize for fiction. He lives in Santa Fe, New Mexico.

The Recipe

This time of year, fruitcakes are among the most despised of American phenomena, right up there with lawyers and street mimes. Actually, some of my best friends are lawyers, and I don't have much to fear from mimes. They are, after all, primarily a big-city infestation. I can't remember seeing a single one the whole time we lived in Conway.

But I have to admit I have an unreasonable bias against fruitcakes. I worry about a dessert with a greater specific gravity than the nickel-iron core of the planet. I'm repelled by the way brilliant bits of jellied fructoid cling to my teeth. I'm suspicious of any supposed digestible which can exist for decades without undergoing any detectable change of state.

But in our family, when I was growing up, we had a variation I purely loved. It was heavy and dark and richly flavored. It had raisins and pecans, but it wasn't overly sweet, and it contained no citron at all. We called it nutcake.

It must have been a fairly inexpensive treat: flour, eggs, butter, sugar, milk. We gathered the eggs from our own chickens—this was back when everybody had chickens. Likely as not the milk was fresh from a church-member's cow, and the butter had been churned that morning, and both had been given to us—an unofficial fringe benefit offsetting the low clergyman's salary. Raisins didn't cost much, and the pecans were free—this was back when you gathered them from your own trees or gleaned them in buckets from the groves after the commercial pickers had finished. Yes, nutcake was cheap, and plentiful, but when it was in season, we thought we ate like kings.

There was only one problem. It was a problem whose solution varied from year to year, calling forth our greatest creative resources. And it was a problem whose solution, I now realize, became one of our fondest annual traditions.

The problem was finding the recipe. Not "the recipe" as in a set of instructions for mixing and baking the delectable, but "the recipe" as in my grandmother's euphemism for the booze, the sauce, the spirits, the liquor. You needed the recipe to flavor the batter in the first place, and then you needed the recipe to soak the completed product, so that it would grow moister and more complex and more wonderfully redolent as it aged.

But we were a preacher's family, remember. A Baptist preacher's family. And as everyone knows, Baptists have a powerful affinity for strong drink, and therefore rate it as prime among evils, ahead of even dancing, playing cards, and wearing natural fibers.

The whole state was dry, so the recipe had to come to us fortuitously, through mysterious channels. We looked for it without looking, we expected it without planning. We had to be patient, and exist in faith: It was Godless alcohol we needed, and we counted on the Lord to provide it. It might be a bottle of Beaujolais a wealthy deacon had brought back from an unusual trip to France, a bottle he handed over explaining that he and his would never drink it. How did he know we needed it? Word got around. Or maybe a bootlegger would leave a jug on the step, his conscience offering for the year. Somehow, back then, I never wondered what happened to the rest of the jug once the nutcakes were all done and wrapped.

One year my grandfather, Doc, came home with most of a fifth of gin, claiming he had found it in the ditch beside the road. And somehow, back then, I never wondered how it might happen that anybody in the Mississippi Delta would toss most of a fifth of gin out the window.

I know what you're thinking. Gin? In a holiday nutcake? Listen, those were the very best nutcakes of all, and I don't think it's just nostalgia speaking.

Nostalgia plays its part, though. Looking back I see that the search for the recipe added as much flavor to our lives as it did to the nutcake. It was our tacit admission of the rest of the truth, our tiny romance with sin. In the days of the Nativity, in the season of the coming of The Spotless One, we giggled and whispered and flirted with the Devil. The recipe was forbidden, and it was OK. It was dangerous, and yet it was perfectly harmless.

We lost my grandfather more than a decade ago. We lost my grandmother just this year, after a long and painful decline. It cannot redeem the suffering of her last decade, but I feel compelled to lift a glass of the recipe as I write this. I feel compelled to say to her, although I think she cannot hear me—so far have I fallen—that I loved her nutcake, that it was Christmas to me.

Granny's Nutcake
    1 lb. (2 cups) sugar
    ½ teaspoon salt
    ½ lb. (1 cup) butter
    2 teaspoons nutmeg
    6 medium eggs
    1 teaspoon cinnamon
    ½ cup black molasses
    1 lb. raisins

4 cups unbleached white flour
6 ounces wine or whisky
1 tsp baking soda
pecans

Total preparation and baking time: about 105 minutes.
1. Preheat oven to 200˚.
2. Let butter soften.
3. Beat together sugar and butter till creamy. Beat in eggs one at a time. Beat in molasses.
4. In another bowl, sift together flour, baking soda, salt, nutmeg, cinnamon.
5. Slowly beat dry mixture into wet. Add raisins and pecans and stir well. Add wine or whisky or other "recipe" and stir with a rubber spatula till smooth.
6. Line bottom of loaf pan or round cake pan with wax paper. Pour in batter.
7. Bake for at least 80 minutes (remember heat is very low), probably longer for loaf pan. Done when a toothpick comes out clean. To store, soak lightly (or heavily) with more of the "recipe."

—Jack Butler

KAYE GIBBONS

Biographical statement, p. 102.

Cold Oven Pound Cake

3 cups flour
3 cups sugar
1 cup milk
2 sticks butter
1/2 cup Crisco
5 eggs
1 ½ teaspoons vanilla
1 teaspoon lemon extract

Cream butter and sugar together. Beat in sugar in small quantities. Add almost half of the flour and the milk, a little at a time. Add eggs, one at a time, with the remainder of the flour. Pour into prepared bundt pan and put into a cold oven. Set oven to 325° and bake 1 hour. Turn oven up to 350° and bake for 30 minutes.

KENNETH HOLDITCH

Biographical statement, p. 12.

Miss Mag's and Mother's Amalgamation Cake

> 2 cups cake flour
> ½ cup Crisco
> ⅔ cup sweet milk
> 1 ¼ cups sugar
> 5 or 6 egg whites
> 2 heaping teaspoons baking powder
> Pinch of salt

(Room temperature for ingredients)
Beat egg whites, not too stiff. Cream Crisco and sugar, then add half of the milk. Then add flour, baking powder gradually, then the rest of the milk. Stir in egg whites with spoon or spatula.

Pour into 3 greased and floured cake pans and bake at 350° for 35 minutes.

Icing
> 6 egg yolks
> 2 cups sugar
> 3 tablespoons flour
> 1 ½ cups coconut juice (or milk)

Beat up real well and cook until it thickens.

Grind:
> 1 large coconut
> 1 cups raisins
> 1 ½ cups nuts (pecans and English walnuts)

Add to mixture along with a piece of butter the size of an egg.

Spread icing between layers. My mother also covered the cake with a seven-minute frosting, which, as it were, added insult to injury.

This recipe, an old Southern favorite, was given to my mother in the late 1930s by Mrs. Buford Smith (Miss Mag) of Ecru, Mississippi. Miss Mag was a wonderful cook and also the first Avon lady in north Mississippi. I have found several recipes for this cake through the years, but this remains the best one to my taste. It is extremely rich and should be served in thin slices.

MARK CHILDRESS

Biographical statement, p. 22.

Dude's Famous Sour-Cream Caramel Cake

Dude (Cranford of Greenville, Alabama) says the Sour-Cream Caramel Cake is "not all that easy to make." I can assure you, though, that it is the best cake I have ever tasted and I am glad she goes to all that trouble.

In keeping with family tradition, this recipe is not particularly slimming.

    2 sticks of butter
    3 cups sugar
    6 eggs, separated
    1 cup sour cream, mixed with ¼ teaspoon baking soda
    3 cups flour
    1 teaspoon vanilla
    Pinch of salt

Whip egg whites until they form soft peaks. Cream butter and sugar until fluffy, then add the egg yolks, one at a time. Alternately stir in the sour cream–soda mixture and the flour. Add the pinch of salt and the vanilla. Fold in the beaten egg whites until well-mixed. Pour into two greased, floured jelly roll pans. Oblong or round cake pans will work fine too. Bake at 325° for 30 minutes, or until toothpick comes out clean. Frost with caramel frosting.

Caramel Frosting
    3 ⅔ cups sugar
    1 ½ cups half-and-half
    1 stick margarine or butter (Dude says she uses oleo because there are already 2 sticks of
        butter in the cake.)

Put ⅔ cup sugar in a heavy boiler over medium-high heat, stirring quite often. Mix 3 cups sugar with the half-and-half, and cook this mixture in another boiler over medium-high heat. The sugar should have turned a nice rich caramel-brown about the time the half-and-half mix is boiling well. Combine the two, add your stick of margarine, and continue boiling until it reaches the soft ball stage (234° to 240° F. on the candy thermometer).

Remove from heat. Let frosting set up for 5 to 10 minutes, stirring occasionally, then frost the cake layers.

Mary Helen's Coca-Cola Cake

My mother, Mary Helen Childress of Slapout, Alabama, got the recipe for Coca-Cola Cake from somebody (we forget who) in the early 1970s. It was a favorite dessert in our family, I think because it contained those other two major Southern food groups—Coke and cake.

Cake
    2 cups flour
    2 cups sugar
    2 sticks butter
    2 tablespoons cocoa powder
    1 cup Coca-Cola
    ½ cup buttermilk
    2 eggs, lightly beaten
    1 teaspoon baking soda
    1 teaspoon vanilla
    1 ½ cups little marshmallows (seriously)

Preheat oven to 350°. Combine sugar and flour. Heat to boiling the butter, cocoa, and Coca-Cola. Pour it over sugar-flour mix. Add buttermilk, eggs, and baking soda. Mix it all together well and bake in a greased, floured, oblong cake pan for 30 to 40 minutes, or until a toothpick comes out clean. Ice the cake while it is still hot.

Icing
    ½ cup butter
    1 tablespoon cocoa powder
    6 tablespoons Coca-Cola
    1 box confectioner's sugar
    1 cup pecans, toasted

Heat the butter, cocoa, and Coke together to a boil. Pour over the powdered sugar and pecans, mix well, and spread over cake.

WYLENE DUNBAR

Biographical statement, p. 44.

Just Right Pumpkin Pie

Pumpkin pie, like potato salad, is a family taste. Pumpkin pies made from other than the family recipe are too bland, too spicy, too lumpy, or the wrong color. This is *my* family's recipe which is, therefore, just right and which, I am told, we copied in 1939 or 1940 from the recipe of "a little old lady in Hutchinson, Kansas, who had a flair for making pies and she entered some contests, won, and it came out in the *Hutchinson News.*" It is not too bland or too spicy and, due to all the beating, has a silken, yet firm, consistency. Pie crust is a logical truth, however, and this one is the truest and best. All Cinnamon Crusts are good, no matter how you make them.

In preparing these recipes, I strictly adhere to my mother's timeless (and rather general) advice: "If you do it right, it will be fine," and it always has been. Also, she told me to use canned pumpkin because "it works better." Having endured a couple of years of growing, seeding, baking, peeling, trimming, mashing, and using "real" pumpkin, I can tell you—it does and it wouldn't matter if it didn't.

> 1 cup sugar
> 1 ¼ cups pumpkin (10-ounce can)
> 2 free-range eggs
> 2 cups whole milk
> 1 teaspoon cinnamon
> ¼ teaspoon cloves
> ¼ teaspoon nutmeg
> ⅛ teaspoon allspice
> ½ teaspoon salt

Beat eggs slightly. Also, beat all lumps out of pumpkin pulp. Add remaining ingredients and eggs to pumpkin. Beat well. Heat milk to scalding point and add a little to pumpkin mixture to make thin enough to pour. Pour pumpkin mixture into remaining milk, while stirring. Pour into 9-inch pie pan, lined with an unbaked shell. Bake at 400° for 50 minutes, or until a table knife inserted 1 inch from center of pie comes out clean.

Best Pie Crust
   3 cups white flour
   1 ¼ cups Fluffo shortening

Cut shortening into flour, using tines of fork or pastry blender, until the size of early peas. Mix together:

   1 free-range egg, beaten
   1 teaspoon cider vinegar
   1 teaspoon salt
   6 tablespoons very cold water

Add to flour mixture and let rest for 10 to 15 minutes. Divide dough and roll out half on floured board to a 10-inch circle. Handle the dough as little and as lightly as possible. Likewise, use as little flour as possible to roll out the dough. Fold rolled-out dough in half and fit into a 9-inch pie pan. Then unfold dough onto other half and flute edge of crust. Use the other half of dough to make cinnamon crusts.

Cinnamon Crusts
Roll out leftover pie dough to ⅛-inch thickness and in abstract shape. Mix together:

   1 cup sugar
   1 teaspoon cinnamon, more or less, according to taste

Pour sugar mixture onto surface of dough and, using palm of hand, spread over entire dough to 1-sugar-grain thickness. Cut in 1 ½-by-3–4 inch strips, leaving ragged edges on the ones at the outside edges of dough. Put on ungreased cookie sheet. Bake at 375° for 12 minutes, or until slightly browned.

GLORIA NORRIS

is the author of a novel and editor of several anthologies. Her short stories have appeared in the *O. Henry Prize Stories* and *The Year's Best: Stories from the South*. She is a native Mississippian.

Lemon Icebox Pie

I grew up in a Mississippi household where a succession of hired cooks jealously ruled the kitchen and guarded their recipes like jewels. On the weekends when they were off, first my grandmother, and later my mother, turned out magnificent Sunday meals. For some reason, none of these excellent cooks wanted a small girl in the kitchen. The result was I went off to college without knowing how to cook anything more substantial than chocolate fudge.

When I found myself at twenty-one in New York City in an apartment with a tiny makeshift kitchen in a closet, I suppose one inspiring outcome might have been that I was spurred to overcome my handicap and transform myself into a seasoned chef who turns out French butter pastry and homemade gnocchi. Instead I continued to be less than a zealous cook. One humble category of food, however, did spur me to mastery in the kitchen and that is pie—chicken pot pie, pecan pie, apple cobbler, pizza pie, quiche. I can and do eat anything by the name of pie for any meal. Not surprisingly, it is from this genre that I developed two dishes that my friends rave over, demand second helpings of, and remember for years. Both were popular during those years when I was banned from the kitchen. I don't think there are any dark psychoanalytic reasons for my mastering these pies while bypassing all the other dishes I was once discouraged from learning to make. These have simply survived as the *madeleines* of my childhood.

This is my culinary *pièce de résistance*. After serving this pie, I have received on-the-spot proposals from all kinds of men—married, single, gay—who want to co-habit with me simply for the chance to regularly eat my pie. No one knows where this cherished old Southern dessert comes from, but I imagine it originated as one of those recipes printed on the labels of the can containing the prime ingredient, in this case, sweetened condensed milk. Judging from its "icebox" title, it came into being around the early years of the century when people kept their perishable foods in simple iceboxs—a tin-lined cabinet with cakes of ice inside.

> 1 can sweetened condensed milk
> Graham crackers
> 1 tablespoon butter or olive oil (optional)

3 large eggs
2 lemons
1 tablespoon sugar

Graham Cracker Crust

When it comes to regular pie pastry, I have nothing against prepared crusts. In fact, I often buy the Pillsbury frozen crusts in a long cylinder that tumble out smooth and beautiful and then plop into a pie pan as though I kneaded and rolled them by hand. But for this pie, don't even consider a store-bought crust. I don't understand why *any*one would be so shameless as to serve those tasteless, dried-out "prepared" graham-cracker crusts in a flimsy foil pan when it's actually more work to go to the store, bring home and unwrap than it is to make a crust from scratch. (My preparation time: about 3 minutes, tops.)

1. Break graham crackers into singles and line up around the edge of a pie pan (for some reason, a glass dish produces a tastier crust). Break crackers as needed to line the bottom with large pieces. Now crumble as many crackers as you need to fill in the many little openings between the larger pieces. Most recipes for graham cracker crusts call for melted butter to hold the crumbs together, but I have never found that necessary. Use your own judgment and add the melted butter or mix crumbs by hand with butter or oil if you like.
2. Set aside.

Lemon Insides

1. Separate the eggs and put the yellows in a large bowl. Set aside the whites in a deep bowl for beating into meringue.
2. Grate the lemons until you have a couple of teaspoons of lemon zest.
3. Cut the same lemons in half and squeeze out the juice. Carefully remove any seeds.
4. Add 2 tablespoons of lemon juice to the condensed milk and stir to blend. Taste to check balance. The lemon flavor grows after the pie sits for a day, so try to take account of that. The tartness will deliciously balance the bland over-sweetness of the condensed milk. If you like a lot of tartness, add a third spoonful. The lemon juice will "cook" the eggs, so cooking time in the oven is minimal.
5. Now add the lemon zest.
6. Add egg yolks and mix.

Meringue Topping

1. Beat the egg whites by hand or electric beater until they easily hold peaks when you mound a spoonful. Be careful not to overbeat since the meringue becomes progressively mushier instead of stiffer.

2. Add 1 tablespoon of sugar and stir through very lightly so as not to disturb that perfectly aerated mass of whites.
3. Mound meringue on top of pie and use your spoon to make attractive peaks.
4. Place in 450° oven and watch carefully, so the peaks brown lightly.
5. Remove and let cool, then cover without squashing the meringue and place in refrigerator. No icebox is needed!

Lemon Icebox Pie tastes best when served 12 to 24 hours after cooking. Then the opposite sweetness and tartness reach a delicious balance. It's wise to make 2 pies since guests' calls for seconds are frequent, and people are really disappointed if you run out.

Buttermilk Pie

This pie goes back to the late eighteenth century in America, according to George Lang, the legendary Hungarian restaurateur who directs the cuisine at the glamorous and historic Café des Artistes restaurant on West 67th Street on Manhattan's West Side. Here artists, literary people, and others have gathered for decades under the famous wall-high murals by Henry Chandler Christie that show nude 1930s-style showgirls pushing each other in swings amid tropical foliage and parrots. Most people notice the girls' beautiful bodies, but as a social anthropologist, I have always enjoyed studying the outmoded hairdo's. The food is famous too, so I was delighted to discover in *The Café des Artistes Cookbook* Lang's recipe for his version of my buttermilk pie, and I was struck that he wrote that it's hard to explain why the simple Buttermilk Pie gives diners "such a feeling of sensuous luxury." I cite Lang's praise along with his declaring its long American lineage to illustrate this is not, as its name might suggest, some cutesy Southern recipe, but a bona fide serious pie of long pan-American heritage and worthy of any table.

Lang marvels that this delicious pie filling is made from only 5 ingredients. My recipe only calls for 4, since I dispense with vanilla flavoring, a wimpy kind of touch-up to any dish in my view.

Usual ingredients for making 9-inch pastry, or use a good prepared frozen substitute. Whichever you choose, be sure you have enough pastry to cover a 9-inch pie dish. The pie contents will overflow a smaller crust.
3 large eggs
1 cup sugar
2 cups low-fat buttermilk (The low-fat buttermilk comes out quite rich, so you need not expend extra calories, but it's up to you.)
1 tablespoon (roughly) of freshly squeezed lemon juice

Pastry

If you make your own, follow your own wisdom. If you use a good frozen crust, as I do, take a few precautions, usually hidden in the fine print on the side of the can or inside the box. Defrost a frozen crust by heating in microwave for 30 seconds at ⅓ power (but not a second more). Prick all over and heat pastry in oven at 450° for 5 minutes (probably 10 minutes for made-from-scratch pastry). This assures the bottom will be done instead of a bit soggy. Be sure to remove on time as frozen crust browns quickly. Lower oven temperature to 350°.

Pie Insides

1. Beat eggs, and add sugar and mix lightly.
2. Add lemon juice and stir through. Test and if you want more lemon juice, add a few drops. As with the Lemon Icebox Pie, the lemon flavor will grow as the pie sits.
3. Add buttermilk and mix.
4. Pour into baked shell.
5. Bake for about 1 hour—but this is a judgment call. After 45 minutes, test for doneness, since sometimes the pie cooks more quickly, depending I suppose on how our planet is spinning. The standard test for pies is to insert a clean knife in the center and if it comes back clean, the pie is done. For myself, I prefer a nonchalant light press of my fingertip here and there on the top. The knife test always produces a slightly overdone pie for me.
6. Let pie cool and then refrigerate 24 hours before serving. This pie definitely needs a day and night chilling in the refrigerator to reach perfection. You can serve some very lightly sweetened whipped crème with this if you like, but I like it plain. Some might stretch this delicious, light, but rich-tasting pie to serve 8, but I would hold it to 6 guests.

Gloria Norris

ANTHONY WALTON

is the author of *Mississippi: An American Journey* and co-editor of *The Vintage Book of African American Poetry: 1750–2000*. He teaches at Bowdoin College.

My Mother's Sweet Potato Pie

This recipe makes 3 pies.

Crust (Bottom only; no top crust)
   2 ¼ cups flour
   1 ½ tablespoons butter
   1 cup Crisco shortening
   1 teaspoon salt
   6 tablespoons cold water

Cut the flour, butter, and shortening together. Add salt. Add water, mixing in 1 tablespoon at a time. Divide the dough into thirds. Roll out each crust, after forming a ball, on wax paper or cutting board.

Filling
   4 sweet potatoes, average size
   3 or 4 eggs
   1 ¼ cups granulated sugar
   2 tablespoons brown sugar
   1 ½ cups butter (3 sticks)
   1 teaspoon nutmeg
   ⅓ cup Carnation milk
   2 tablespoons vanilla

The eggs and butter should be at room temperature. Boil the sweet potatoes, with the skins on. When soft enough to mash, remove from water and peel. Mash the potatoes—picking out strings if potatoes are stringy. This should yield about 2 ½ cups. Add the eggs, stirring in 1 at a time, mixing thoroughly. Add the granulated sugar, mix. Add the brown sugar, mix. Stir in the butter. Add the nutmeg, milk, and vanilla extract, stirring after each addition.

Spoon the mixture into the 3 pie crusts. Bake at 350° or 375° until solid and brown, about 45 minutes to 1 hour. Serve hot or cold.

This Southern classic is a recipe that my mother, Dorothy, learned from watching and working with her mother during her childhood in Mississippi. The recipe has been handed down in like fashion, with individual (often closely guarded) variations, for many generations, and remains a solid favorite of friends and family.

LEE SMITH

Biographical statement, p. 16.

Bourbon-Chocolate-Pecan Pie

¾ cup (4.5 ounces) semisweet chocolate morsels
3 large eggs, lightly beaten
⅓ cup sugar
3 tablespoons firmly packed light brown sugar
1 tablespoon all-purpose flour
¾ cup light corn syrup
¼ cup butter or margarine, melted
3 tablespoons bourbon
2 teaspoons vanilla
2 cups pecan halves

Beat eggs and all other ingredients except pecans together. Put pecans into prepared 9-inch pie pan fitted with pastry crust. Pour mixture over pecans. Bake at 350° for 55 minutes.

Garnish with soft vanilla ice cream or with whipped cream.

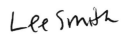

SANDRA BROWN

is the author of more than fifty-five books, including *The Crush*, *Prime Time*, *Sunset Embrace*, and *French Silk Pie*. She resides in Arlington, Texas.

French Silk Pie

I'm always amused when someone asks me to contribute a recipe to a cookbook. I'm the world's worst cook. Furthermore, I'm disinclined to improve my skills. My rule of thumb: if a recipe has more than five ingredients, I forget it.

I broke that rule for this recipe.

I saw French Silk Pie on a dessert menu and, like the confection, the words were so seductive I used them for a book title! While doing my "research" I asked around until a chef was generous enough to share the following recipe.

> 1 stick margarine, room temperature
> ¾ cup sugar
> 1 square Baker's chocolate, melted
> Shaved bitter chocolate or nuts
> 1 teaspoon vanilla
> 2 eggs
> Whipping cream

Cream margarine and sugar. Add chocolate and vanilla. Blend in eggs 1 at a time no less than 3 minutes each. Pour in baked pie shell or graham cracker crust. Let set in refrigerator at least 5 hours before serving. Spread with whipped cream and sprinkle shaved chocolate or nuts over top.

BARRY MOSER

has illustrated, written, or designed over 250 books. His edition of *Alice's Adventures in Wonderland* won the American Book Award for design and illustration in 1983. He teaches at Smith College.

Peaches and Sweet Dumplings

In memory of Willie

8 or 9 fresh peaches, peeled
2 sticks of butter, more or less
Biscuit dough (your own recipe or Bisquick)
1 cup all purpose flour, more or less
1 cup granulated sugar, more or less
3 jiggers peach liqueur or 1 skinny jigger Bourbon whiskey
Pinch of salt, more or less
Water

This is a variation on my Aunt Gracie's recipe for peach cobbler. It works wonderfully well with fresh berries of all sorts, especially dewberries and blackberries, though strawberries not so much. However, apples are mighty tasty done up this way. Like writing or making illustrations for books, imagination reigns, so don't let these instructions inhibit you any. This ain't a complicated preparation, despite the length of the recipe.

Start by peeling 8 or 9 fresh peaches and slicing them into a large mixing bowl. Georgia Belles are perfect for this preparation, but others will do as well, even the poor excuses grown in The Kingdom of the Yankee or California. I have been told you can do it with canned fruit but I don't believe it.

To the sliced peaches add a cup of sugar (more or less, to taste), 3 jiggers peach liqueur (more or less, to taste—and remember that Bourbon works well too, but go easy on it; in fact, take a sip of the jigger and put the rest in the peaches. If you are using fresh berries, use something like Grand Marnier or Cointreau.) Add a pinch of salt and enough water to cover the peaches. Stir the mixture until most of the sugar is dissolved. Set aside. (NOTE: If you use apples, add some cinnamon and cloves, to taste, and a squeeze of a lemon.)

Preheat the oven to 400°.

While the oven's warming, make up some of your favorite biscuit dough. If you don't have such a recipe in your haversack of culinary tricks use Bisquick and follow the directions for making biscuits. No matter what recipe you use, add a few tablespoons of granulated sugar to the mixture.

Turn the sticky dough out on a floured pastry cloth or onto a floured counter top or large cutting board. Sift a bit of flour on top and then turn the ball of dough back onto itself several times until it's smooth and you can pick it up without it sticking to your fingers.

Roll out the dough with a rolling pin (or mash it flat with your hands) into a slab that is about ½ inch thick. Cut the flattened dough into dumplin's 4 or 5 inches long and about as wide as your thumb. (This is not critical. You can cut them any size you wish, and if you do this you can skip the rolling out part and just drop the unfloured, raw dough onto the pan as described below. The more surface area you have, however, the more of the fruit juices will be absorbed and the soupier and yummier the final product will be.)

Butter the bottom of a baking dish with a generous amount of butter—half a stick or so. If you use a shallow dish, the cooking time will be considerably shortened. Use good judgment. Personally, I prefer a deeper pan. I have also made this preparation in individual ramekins (or small aluminum pans for picnics), but be warned—it cooks pretty quickly in small amounts. No matter, lots of butter on the bottom is essential.

Lay strips of the dough on the bottom of the buttered pan, leaving an inch or so of space between, or just drop the dough from a spoon in golf-ball sized dollops. It makes no real difference except to the appearance of the dish. You can even basket-weave long strips if you want to spend the time.

Stir the peaches and the juices and pour over the dumplings. If you are doing a shallow dish this may be sufficient, but if you are using a deeper dish you want to add a second layer of dumplin's. Add more of the peaches and all the juices so that everything is just about covered.

Cut a stick of butter into patties and place them evenly around the top. Place in the middle of the hot oven and let it bake for about 45 minutes. The baking time will, of course, vary according to how deep a dish you have made. Keep an eye on it. It's done when the dumplin's are thoroughly cooked. This dish rises a good bit, so be prepared: put the baking dish on a cookie sheet covered in tinfoil. It'll save a sticky and tenacious mess to have to clean up later.

Remove the Peaches and Sweet Dumplings from the oven and let them sit for half an hour or so. Serve them warm in soup bowls topped with vanilla ice cream (cheddar cheese on the apples will make your tongue lay over.)

If you still have some bourbon left it makes a mighty fine accompaniment.

Praise Jesus. (optional)

CLIFTON L. TAULBERT

was born in the Mississippi Delta and has written nine books, including the Pulitzer-nominated *The Last Train North* and *Once upon a Time When We Were Colored*. He lives in Tulsa, Oklahoma.

Southern Peach Cobbler

Remembered & Tried miles and miles from the First Taste

This recipe starts out with conversation, laughter and memory as all southern delicacies do. As a southern writer with a vivid memory and an even greater sense of taste and smell, I have carried with me around the world, my memory of what a legitimate "Peach Cobbler" should look like and how it should smell and taste. My memory takes me back to my great aunt's kitchen in the Mississippi Delta where her contribution to my health and continued well-being was her quickly put-together "Peach-Cobbler." Mama Ponk, as she was affectionately known will not go down in southern history as an extraordinary cook, but for me, the young boy who tugged at her apron strings, her "Peach Cobbler" will always remain a winner. The problem is I never saw her cook the cobbler from start to finish. So I have carried this idea around of how I think her masterful feat was accomplished. And while single and living on my own many years ago, I perfected my version of this quickly put-together and tasty cobbler.

Ingredients

Courage & Desire
A kitchen with no one but you in the space
A radio with the ability to still play the sounds of Ruth Brown and Hank Snow
[Note: Our radio could only get the combined blues and country music station]
You must wear blue jeans and a good white shirt with no holes
An oven suitable baking dish
[Your hunger desire determines the size—be reasonable]
Lots of real butter—at least two whole sticks
Mix a cup of white sugar and brown sugar and shake to the music
Have real Pet Milk standing by
Frozen peaches—frozen in syrup

Nutmeg
Cinnamon
One can of baking biscuits
[I recalled crust and inside dumplings, but had no idea how to duplicate, so I improvised]
Clean your baking dish—this is very important

PUTTING IT TOGETHER
Split each can of biscuit in half and layer the bottom of the dish
Cover with the mixed sugar
Sprinkle spices
Just cover with thick slices of butter
Pour just a little of the Pet Milk—just to cover the top
Next, cover with peaches
Repeat—the biscuits, sugar, spices, butter, no milk
One more time—cover with peaches
Repeat the biscuits, sugar, spices, butter, milk
Place in a preheated oven 350° and cook until the smell wraps around you
[cook from 40 to 50 minutes]

Clifton L. Taulbert

BARBARA BUSH

Biographical statement, p. 34.

Red, White, and Blue Cobbler
(Serves 6)

    1 can blueberry pie filling
    1 can cherry pie filling

Place blueberry pie filling in bottom of 8-by-8-inch glass baking pan. Spread evenly and then place the cherry pie filling on top, smoothing to edges of pan. Place in 400° oven to heat while preparing topping.

Topping
    1 cup flour
    1 tablespoon sugar
    1 ½ teaspoons baking powder
    ½ teaspoon salt
    3 tablespoons shortening
    ½ cup milk

Mix dry ingredients and shortening until mixture is like fine crumbs. Stir in milk and drip by spoonfuls onto hot filling. Bake at 400° for 25 to 30 minutes or until brown. Serve topped with vanilla ice cream . . . or try homemade recipe that follows.

Homemade Filling
    • Blueberry Filling
    ¼ cup sugar
    ½ tablespoon cornstarch
    ½ teaspoon lemon juice
    2 cups fresh or frozen unsweetened blueberries

    • Cherry Filling
    1 can sour pie cherries
    ½ cup plus 2 tablespoons sugar

1 ½ tablespoons cornstarch
⅛ teaspoon cinnamon
⅛ teaspoon almond extract

Blueberry Filling: Mix sugar and cornstarch in a saucepan and add all other ingredients. Cook until thickened. Put into 8-by-8-inch pyrex pan and keep hot in a 250° oven while making cherry filling.

Cherry Filling: In a saucepan, mix dry ingredients. Gradually stir in juice from canned cherries and cook until thickened, adding cherries and flavorings at the end. Smooth cherry filling over blueberry mixture. Keep hot while making topping.

Barbara Bush

ROSELLEN BROWN

Biographical statement, p. 78.

World's Simplest Torte

This is so good and fast and simple that I feel it my duty to spread the word.

1 scant cup sugar

½ cup shortening

2 eggs

1 cup flour

1 teaspoon baking powder

Fruit for topping, with cinnamon and sugar if appropriate, fresh or canned; or chocolate sauce—whatever comes to hand

Cream sugar and shortening. Beat in eggs. Combine dry ingredients and add to mixture; beat a few minutes more. (For a lighter cake, whip whites separately and fold in.) Pour into greased pan—this is good in a round layer cake pan, a pie plate, or a tube pan. Top with just about anything. You can cut in chocolate sauce to make a marble cake, arrange fruit neatly or throw it on loosely. Bake at 350° until firm but not stiff. Do not overbake.

The torte will be fairly thin and firm—it is not spongy. It takes no time to assemble and can be topped with just about anything, and an added layer of ice cream never hurt it. It's a real lifesaver when you're rushed.

JOHN EGERTON

is a journalist and author whose books include *Shades of Gray, Visions of Utopia,* and *Speak Now against the Day: The Generation before the Civil Rights Movement in the South,* which received the Robert F. Kennedy Book Award. He lives in Nashville, Tennessee.

Huguenot Torte and Ozark Pudding

The Huguenot torte, a delectable nut and apple pudding-cake topped with whipped cream, is widely appreciated in the South Carolina low country as a classic Charleston dessert of historical significance.

Like the great English trifles that have been served at Virginia dining tables for almost four centuries, Huguenot tortes are often touted as original confections from the mother country.

Huguenots—French Protestants seeking religious freedom—were among the earliest and most influential of Charleston's seventeenth-century settlers. That the rich and irresistible dessert bearing their name dates back to that period makes a believable story. The promotional materials extolling the city's historic and contemporary virtues as much as say so, and modern cookbooks from the region do too.

But John Taylor, the irrepressible owner of Hoppin' John's, a cookbook specialty shop in Charleston, has come up with information indicating that the beloved torte is a mid-twentieth-century creation strikingly similar to an Arkansas-Missouri mountain sweet called Ozark pudding.

Writing in *Omnibus,* a Charleston-area monthly, Taylor declares that "Charleston's famous 'torte' is not a torte at all," not 200 or more years old, and not even French; *au contraire,* it is "probably a twentieth-century conceit" borrowed from the landlocked upper South.

He backs up this bold assertion with impressive facts. First, there are no Huguenot torte recipes in South Carolina cookbooks prior to World War II. Second, a recipe for Ozark pudding very similar to the standard formula for Huguenot torte was served at a dinner in honor of Winston Churchill and Harry Truman in Fulton, Missouri, in 1946.

Third, Taylor interviewed Evelyn Anderson Florance, whose Huguenot torte recipe was published in the 1950 Junior League classic, *Charleston Receipts,* and learned that her inspiration for the dessert had come from an Ozark pudding she ate at a church supper in Galveston, Texas, in the 1930s.

"I got a recipe for it," said Mrs. Florance, "and worked with it until it was the way I liked it." She named it Huguenot torte in about 1942, she added, when she was asked to make desserts for a Charleston restaurant called the Huguenot Tavern.

So, it wasn't seventeenth-century French Huguenots who gave Charleston its celebrated tortes; it was Evelyn Florance, a contemporary Junior Leaguer, borrowing from an Ozark Mountain tradition in another part of the South.

Or was it? For the question still remains: Where did the Ozark pudding recipes served in Texas and Missouri come from, and also the one in *The Progressive Farmer's Southern Cookbook* (1961), which is the earliest one I can find in print?

Though *The Progressive Farmer* book calls it "an Arkansas favorite," I could find almost no mention of Ozark pudding in the old cookbooks of that state—or, for that matter, in Missouri's. Apparently, the dessert was as uncommon in yesterday's Ozarks as Huguenot torte was in the Carolina low country of long ago.

So if Huguenot torte was inspired by an Ozark pudding recipe in the 1930s, what or who inspired the first Ozark pudding?

It may be impossible to answer that question with any assurance, but I have a candidate to nominate. *Southern Cooking*, by Mrs. S. R. Dull of Atlanta, first published in 1928, includes a recipe called Apple Torte that contains exactly the same ingredients (in slightly different proportions) as the Huguenot torte in *Charleston Receipts* and the Ozark pudding in *The Progressive Farmer's Southern Cookbook*.

Not from the mother country, then, but from good old Mother Dull. If she does in fact deserve credit for having put both Huguenot torte and Ozark pudding into the South's culinary repertoire, that's hardly news; Henrietta Stanley Dull and her classic cookbook gave much that is original and lasting to Southern cookery.

Here, for the record, is Mrs. Dull's Apple Torte, a confection worthy of the best tables from Charleston to the Ozarks.

Beat 2 eggs well and add 1 cup of sugar, ½ tablespoon of flour, 1 ½ teaspoons of baking powder, ⅛ teaspoon of salt, 1 teaspoon of vanilla extract, ½ cup of chopped nuts (ideally, black walnuts), and 1 cup of chopped apples (use firm, tart apples, peeled). When thoroughly mixed, pour into a well-greased shallow pan or dish (about 8-by-12 inches) and bake at 350° for 30 minutes.

Serve warm with whipped cream. And while you're eating it, say a little silent word of thanks for the Huguenots and the mountaineers—and especially for dear old Mother Dull, who was a pretty sharp lady.

John Egerton

CYNTHIA SHEARER

teaches writing at the University of Mississippi, where she also served as curator of William Faulkner's home, Rowan Oak. She is the author of *The Wonder Book of the Air* and is completing her second novel, *The Celestial Jukebox.*

Pignoli

4 ounces Pignolia (for you Southerners, "pine nuts")
8 ounces canned almond paste, cut into small pieces
⅔ cup sugar
2 egg whites
1 teaspoon lemon peel, fresh, grated

Preheat oven to 325° F. Line a cookie sheet with foil, parchment, or heavy brown paper. Place pine nuts in shallow dish. In medium-size bowl beat almond paste, sugar, egg whites, and lemon peel with electric mixer until smooth. With slightly wet hands form dough into 1-inch balls, using a heaping teaspoon for each. Press balls into nuts, flattening balls slightly and coating one side. Place 1 inch apart on prepared cookie sheet. Bake 22 to 25 minutes until golden brown.

Cool completely on cookie sheet or rack. Store tightly covered. Keeps 2 weeks.

Cynthia Shearer

ALLAN GURGANUS

is the author of *Oldest Living Confederate Widow Tells All, White People, Plays Well with Others,* and *The Practical Heart.* He received the Sue Kaufman Prize from the American Academy of Arts and Letters. He lives in North Carolina.

Take, Eat, These Are My Jesus Cookies
(a holy week baking project for you and the kids)

This is my favorite recent recipe. It was published first by an Episcopal congregant in a church-sponsored cookbook sold for support of the building fund.

> 1 cup pecan halves
> 1 teaspoon vinegar
> 3 egg whites
> Pinch of salt
> 1 cup sugar
> Ziploc bag
> Wooden spoon
> Tape
> Bible

Preheat oven to 300°. Place pecans in Ziploc bag and let children beat them with the wooden spoon to break into small pieces. Explain that after Jesus was arrested he was beaten by Roman soldiers. (Read John 19:1–3.) Let each child smell the vinegar. Put 1 teaspoon vinegar into mixing bowl. Explain that when Jesus was thirsty on the cross he was given vinegar to drink. (Read John 19:28–30.) Add egg whites to the vinegar. Eggs represent life. Explain that Jesus gave his life to give us life. (Read John 10:10–11.) Sprinkle a little salt into each child's hand. Let them taste it and brush the rest into the bowl. Explain that this represents the salty tears shed by Jesus' followers, and the bitterness of our own sin. (Read Luke 23:27.) So far the ingredients are not very appetizing. Add 1 cup sugar. Explain that the sweetest part of the story is that Jesus died because he loves us. He wants us to know and belong to him. (Read Psalm 34:8 and John 3:16.) Beat ingredients with a mixer on high speed 12 to 15 minutes until stiff peaks are formed. Explain that the color white represents the purity in God's eyes of those whose sins have been cleansed by Jesus. (Read Isaiah 1:18 and John 3:1–3.) Fold in broken nuts. Drop by teaspoon onto wax paper-covered cookie sheet. Explain that each mound represents the rocky tomb where Jesus' body was laid. (Read Matthew 27:57–60.) Put the cookie sheet in the oven. Close the door and turn the oven off. Give each child a piece of tape and seal the oven door. Explain that Jesus' tomb was sealed. (Read Matthew 27:65–66.) GO TO BED!! Explain that they may feel sad to leave the cookies in the oven overnight. Jesus' followers were in despair when the tomb was sealed. (Read John 16:20–22.) On Easter morning, open the oven and give everyone a cookie. Notice the cracked surface and take a bite. The cookies are hollow. On the first Easter Jesus' followers were amazed to find the tomb open and empty. (Read Matthew 28:1–9.)

Allan Gurganus

ANN FISHER-WIRTH

Biographical statement, p. 181.

Aunt Joanie's Toffee Bars

  1 cup butter
  1 cup packed brown sugar
  1 egg yolk
  1 teaspoon vanilla
  2 cups flour
  1 8-ounce bar milk chocolate (Hershey's works best)
  ½ cup nuts, chopped

Preheat oven to 300°. Mix the first four ingredients. Add flour. Spread in a greased 13-by-10-inch pan. Bake 20 to 25 minutes. Melt chocolate on top of the stove and spread over the bars while warm. Sprinkle with nuts. Cut into bars. These are my family's favorite cookies at Christmastime.

Ann Fisher-Wirth

BOBBIE ANN MASON

has held a Guggenheim Fellowship and a National Endowment for the Arts grant. Her works include *Shiloh, Feather Crowns,* and *Clear Springs,* a finalist for the Pulitzer Prize. She lives in central Kentucky.

Boiled Custard

4 cups milk
2 or 3 eggs, beaten thoroughly
⅓ cup sugar
2 teaspoons vanilla
Pinch of salt
Nutmeg

Put milk and salt in double boiler on high heat. Stir in sugar until it dissolves. Stir in beaten eggs gradually as milk heats. Begin adding them while milk is warm, not too hot. It's best to pour the eggs in from a measuring cup, slowly, in a thin stream while stirring the milk with the other hand. Cook the mixture, stirring until it coats the spoon. Remove from double boiler and stir in vanilla. Cool. Serve cold, with a sprinkling of grated nutmeg.

Boiled custard is usually served at Christmas, with cake. It is a thick liquid, similar to eggnog, but thicker, and it has a different flavor because the eggs are cooked.

Making the custard will require some trial and error and tasting. Knowing when the mixture coats the spoon is a subtle thing. Tasting it and recognizing when the eggs are cooked will be your best guide. It is best to beat the eggs well, even in a blender, in order to avoid lumps of boiled egg—unless you like it that way. The amount of sugar is also variable, to taste. One tablespoon per cup is fine with me.

This was my grandmother's recipe. She insisted on making it with country eggs, not store-bought eggs. Real country eggs are yellow when cooked, not pale. Boiled custard is a specific for the sick, especially if you are a child.

If you separate the eggs and beat the whites, you can make a floating island. Add the egg whites to the hot liquid at the end, when you're ready to remove the pan from the boiler. You can fold the whites in or spoon them on top and let them float. They should cook in their custard bath.

The first time I ever made boiled custard was when I was in graduate school, living on my own and knowing nothing about cooking. I got a craving for this comfort food, and I made it by instinct. And I succeeded in making it, with carefully hand-beaten egg whites sep-arated and folded in. I cooled it and chilled it and then prepared to enjoy this exquisite treat. That's when I discovered that I had mistakenly and inexplicably used salt instead of sugar. I was undaunted, though. The craving for this food from home was so strong that I started all over again and carefully reconstructed the dish, this time with sugar. It was perfect.

Bobbie Ann Mason

JAYNE ANNE PHILLIPS

Biographical statement, p. 23.

Jane Jr. Ice Cream Salad

My recipe, to make with kids three and up

   2 packages Jello (flavor of choice)
   2 cups boiling water
   1 quart ice cream
   1 cup cold water or juice

Dissolve Jello in boiling water; stir in ice cream and water or juice. And don't even think of adding fruit. They don't like it with chunks.

DAVID MADDEN

Biographical statement, p. 134.

Fig Ice Cream

Cranking ice cream is one of my favorite eating memories of summer Sunday dinners at the home place. Maraschino cherry, rum raisin, strawberry, banana, but seldom vanilla or chocolate. Gran'paw made us crank until our arms were sore and the last turn took about a minute—hard, hard, hard as a rock, he insisted, and then he beat his own dish of it soft and ate it with cornbread. My big brother hid himself, partly because he got an ice cream headache. My little brother whined, but was first in line with a bowl. So that's me, under the oak tree that later fell on the roof, almost twirling—it's all in the wrist—the handle at the outset, but then the sweat hits the handle-paddle housing, and then, as it gets hard, I'm dancing into the turning action.

I became an ice-cream maker eccentric, in experiments with ingredients (3 pints of cream, 3 oranges, and 3 bananas—no sugar) and in rituals (cooling the can in the ice before dumping in the mixture for the big push). Once I threw a picnic for my students in Boone, North Carolina, high up in the mountains, and Maurice Stirewalt, worn out from cranking, asked me if it was done yet. "Hell, no, this is just where we get the can cold. Here's the ingredients." He was furious and then hysterical with laughter and never gets tired telling the story. No storytelling from me, just bossing everybody within reach of my voice, telling everybody exactly what to do on a very strict time schedule, making everybody happy at last, though. Especially with my Louisiana innovation: Fig Ice Cream.

One morning, setting the trash out in the alley, I discovered a fig tree with actual ripe figs on it. Their delicately sweet nectar inspired me to try it with cream. Last night, for me and my wife, Robbie, this is how I did it: I mixed one pint half and half with a cup of sugar while Robbie slowly split—the way Glenda Jackson did in that great erotic scene in *Women in Love*—the fresh figs and skinned them and, instead of licking them into her mouth like Glenda, gently mashed the lovely innards with a fork and set them aside. To speed up the freezing action induced by the rock salt acting upon the ice, I pour in a glass of water as a conducting agent. (I think I know what I am talking about here.)

When the cranking turns resistant to a certain degree, I carefully remove the housing, while Robbie keeps her finger on the rim of the can to keep it from floating out of its socket in the bottom of the wooden barrel. Yes, it's soft, so I dump in the figs. And that's it. Except the hard work down to the finish. Not to mention the incredibly lovely delicate fig meat and nectar in the ice basic cream that your lips, your tongue, the cave of your mouth, even your teeth—risking ice cream headache—savor the taste and velvet touch of.

David Madden

ADRIANA TRIGIANI

grew up in Virginia and now lives in New York City. A playwright, television writer, and documentary filmmaker, she is the author of three novels: *Big Stone Gap, Big Cherry Holler,* and *Milk Glass Moon.*

Cousin Dee's Peanut-Butter Balls

This recipe appears in Big Cherry Holler.

One of my first culinary memories of Big Stone Gap, Virginia, was tasting a peanut-butter ball sold by a first-grade Halloween Princess candidate at Big Stone Gap Elementary School. The confection came in a twist of saran wrap, two for ten cents. (Ten cents was a lot of dough back in the 1970s.) It seemed every girl in school was running for princess, and every mother had made her best cookie or candy to sell to raise the funds necessary to secure the royal crown. There were princess candidates who hustled cupcakes (how boring), candy apples (too unwieldy for recess eating), and divinity candy (too delicate for distribution and too blah for my taste), and yes, they were determined to unload their inventory and win— but it was the girl with the peanut-butter balls who had a line across the playground. It's fair to say that peanut-butter balls were the best seller.

There is something mystic about the peanut-butter ball, a milk chocolate orb with a creamy peanut-butter center. On my first book tour in the year 2000, I discovered that the peanut-butter ball had many variations nationwide, and many names. My favorite alternate name is "buckeye," made with delight by our Ohio sisters. And yes, it does look like a buckeye that falls from the trees, but rounder.

I hope you enjoy this recipe that comes your way by my pal Dee Emmerson, an Alabama girl I met at the Milbank Boarding House for women in 1983. She makes peanut-butter balls around the holidays and almost got evicted from her apartment when she poured the excess hot paraffin down her kitchen sink and clogged her building's plumbing. Ah well, a small price to pay for the best candy you'll ever taste. Here goes—and don't think there won't soon be a bed for peanut-butter ball-aholics at Betty Ford. You can't eat just one.

Blend: 1 box of confectioner's sugar
18-ounce jar of crunchy peanut butter
2 cups of graham cracker crumbs
2 sticks of melted butter

Roll into bite-size balls.
Melt: 12-ounce package of semisweet chocolate chips
¼ box paraffin wax
Dip balls into melted chocolate and wax and place on wax paper.

Adriana Trigiani

WILLIAM KENNEDY

won the Pulitzer Prize and the National Book Critics Circle Award for Fiction for his novel *Ironweed*. He is the author of *Legs*, *The Flaming Corsage*, and *Billy Phelan's Greatest Game*. He lives in Averill Park, New York.

Negative Cooking, Negative Eating

Negative Cooking

I discovered negative cooking when I was eight and required a radical infusion of chocolate fudge. "Impossible," said my grandmother, "we don't have the ingredients." I found recipes in two cookbooks and saw, if I combined elements of both, we did have the ingredients. I combined, and set the finished product in the fridge, where it did not harden for six weeks, unusual for fudge. This proved two things to me: I could not cook, and was pervaded by an unreal sense of hope.

Negative Eating (Part One)

Take from fridge or vegetable bin all celery and peppers, raw or cooked, all zucchini, and cucumbers of any kind except when they are dark green dill pickles. Put these all out on the porch so they do not contaminate the next step.

   Bring onto the counter all cheeses in the fridge.

Historical Interlude

I did not eat cheese until I was twenty-seven, when I tasted Kraft's pineapple cheese spread and did not die from the odor or taste. This is cheese infancy. I ate only pineapple spread for seven years, at which point I was getting off the night city desk of the *Albany Times-Union* at 2 A.M. and had had no dinner. I found my way to Joey Russell's bar (he called it Ed's Bar) with my imagination focused on a can of beef stew that sat eternally dusty on a shelf above the gin. I asked Joey for the stew but he said he had no way to cook it. "Why do you keep it on the bar?" I asked him. "Why did I get married?" he asked me. He said the only food in the place was saltine crackers, Swiss cheese, and mustard. "I'll try it," I said. I cut a small piece of Swiss and put it in the middle of a cracker, covered it with mustard, and ate it all at once to disguise the cheese. I did not die or retch. I ate all cheese, all crackers, asked for more, thus gave up pineapple spread forever, and entered cheese puberty. Two years later in the Knights of Columbus bowling alley, I found myself drinking beer and eating Limburger cheese, which smells, depending on room temperature, like either terminal halitosis or diseased dog kidneys. But it tastes better than both, and perceiving this, I entered cheese manhood.

Negative Eating (Part Two)

Unwrap all cheese you put on the counter, taste each, with fragment of French *baguette*. If you do not have a *baguette*, or if your cholesterol is over 250, book passage to Paris and go to *La Muniche* on Left Bank and order *Espinoisses*, a runny, quintuple cream cheese. They have *baguettes* at *La Muniche*. On following day, hire car and drive to Trianon Palace at Versailles, go to lunch, order Bordeaux wine (*rouge*), eat, wait for cheese cart to visit your table as finale. Study eighty-five cheeses offered. Eat any or, eventually, all, depending on how much dessert you've had. Do not worry about cholesterol. Cholesterol is a negative eating factor in America but French people have no cholesterol, a consequence of drinking Bordeaux wine and smoking Galouise cigarettes. The French also are either of average weight or underweight, and since the French Revolution no one has died of cheese.

Return to America without cheese. Resume life at an inferior level of *fromage*. This is American cheese maturity. Keep your passport up to date for cheese emergencies.

William Turner

Cooking is easy if you know how to read.

— ELLEN GILCHRIST

INDEX

Alan Lightman

Anna Quindlen

Fannie Flagg

Barbara Bush   K. Abbott

Josephine Humphreys   Ann Fisher-Wirth

Tony Hillerman

Anne Rapp

Jayne Anne Phillips

Allan Gurganus

Thom Jones

Howard Norman

Steve Hoar   Jill McCorkle

John Berendt   Dave Barry   Bailey White

E. Annie Proulx

Rick Bass